The Origin and History of the Doctrine of Endless Punishment

Eternal Hellfire as Pagan Belief, the Bible's Word on Sheol, and the New Testament Doctrine

By Thomas B. Thayer

Prove all things. Hold fast that which is good. - PAUL

Published by Pantianos Classics

ISBN-13: 978-1-78987-229-3

First published in 1855

Contents

Preface

This little work is written for the purpose of furnishing a sketch of the argument by which it is shown that the doctrine of Endless Punishment is not of divine origin, but traceable directly to a heathen source.

It is not intended as an elaborately philosophical or critical discussion of the subject, as the size of the volume will show; but only as a popular presentation of the method of proof, and of the leading facts and authorities on which the argument rests.

Those having time and sources of information at command, will enter into a more thorough investigation for themselves. For such this work is not designed; but for those who, not having the opportunity, nor the books, necessary to a complete and critical examination of the question, wish a brief statement of the facts and arguments on which is grounded the assertion that the doctrine of endless torments is of heathen origin.

This will account for the absence of many things which the reader might justly expect to find here, and which rightfully claim place in a work bearing the title of this.

The subject treated is one of very great importance, and equally concerns the purity of Christian doctrine, and the happiness and virtue of those believing. It is every day commanding more and more attention from serious and thoughtful minds. And on all sides, and in the churches of all sects, there is increased inquiry into the foundations of the doctrine, and rapidly growing doubts of its divine origin and authority. It is possible the following pages may help to answer some of the questions growing out of this state of mind, and to show how a doctrine, thoroughly heathen in origin and character, came to be adopted by the Christian church.

The sale of the first edition of nearly two thousand copies in the space of three or four months, without being advertised in any form, has encouraged me to believe that the work meets an actual want, and will be serviceable to the cause of Truth. In the preparation of the present edition, therefore, I have made considerable additions; and, I trust, improvements also, in the hope of making it more worthy and more useful. Two chapters and two sections entire have been added, and chapters three, four and six, have been greatly enlarged, and the argument illustrated and fortified by new facts and authorities.

Still the book is far from what I could wish, or what it might be made, if time, and all the means of investigation, were at command. Yet, such as it is, I send it forth again, to do what work it may; believing that, in the conflict of opinions, Truth only is immortal, and cheerfully confident, therefore, that, at last, all error and all evil will perish.

Since the above was written, this work has passed through several large editions. The present issue has additional testimonies strengthening the argument in its various branches. Most of these, with the exception of those pertaining to Chapters III and IX., which are inserted in the body of the text, are gathered into a single chapter at the end of the book; and to facilitate reference, notes have been added to the chapters and sections to which they severally belong.

Boston, January, 1871.

Chapter One - The Period Before the Law

The following two positions will be admitted without question, it is believed, by all Christians.

1st. If the doctrine of endless punishment be, as affirmed by its believers, absolutely and indispensably necessary to the preservation of virtue, and to perfect obedience to the laws of God; if this be the salutary and saving influence of the doctrine, then it constitutes one of the strongest possible reasons for its being revealed to man at the very earliest period of the world's history.

2d. If endless punishment be true, it is terribly true to all those who are in danger, - wherein is found another powerful reason why it should have been made known in the clearest manner, on the very morning of creation! *In the clearest manner:* it should not have been left in doubt, and obscurity, by the use of indefinite terms; but it should have been proclaimed in language which no man *could* misunderstand, if he would. Rather than that there should even be the possibility of a mistake in a matter of such vast and fearful moment, it should have been graven by special miracle into every soul that God sent into the world.

Let us, then, proceed to inquire if we have any such revelation of the doctrine. When God created Adam and Eve, and placed them in the garden of Eden, did He announce to them any law for their observance, having attached to it the penalty in question? Surely justice demanded, if He had forced them into being subject to this awful peril, that He should set out before them both the law and its punishment in the most specific manner. Did He do this? Where is the record of it? Read diligently the first and second chapters of Genesis, and see if anything of this sort is recorded there, in connection with the creation of man.

In chapter ii 15-17, we have this statement: "And the Lord God took the man, and put him into the garden of Eden to dress it and keep it. And the Lord God commanded the man, saying, Of every tree of the garden thou mayest freely eat, but of the tree of the knowledge of good and evil, thou shalt not eat of it: for in the day that thou eatest thereof thou shalt surely die."

This is the only record we have bearing on the subject; but there is no moral law here, which is declared as the future rule of life for them, and for all their posterity. They are simply commanded not to eat of the forbidden tree. Now, whether this is understood in a literal or allegorical sense, we cannot suppose that we have here the formal announcement of a divine law, which claimed the obedience of all mankind on the penalty of endless torment. We certainly cannot believe that God would open the great drama of our life on this earth, involving such infinite consequences, in such brief and

doubtful language, and with so little specification where so much was needed.

As regards the penalty of disobeying the commandment, do we find any statement which can be mistaken for endless punishment? God says, "In the day thou eatest thereof thou shalt surely die;" but this is very far from saying, "Thou shalt, after the death of the body, be subjected to the torments of an endless hell."

We are told, to be sure, that this means "death temporal, death spiritual, and death eternal;" but where is the proof of it? So terrible a doctrine must not be assumed, but demonstrated by unquestionable evidence. Who can believe that God would reveal so frightful a punishment in language so easily misunderstood - by the single word "die," a term employed in such a variety of senses, capable of such a wide latitude of usage?

Would any earthly parent, if the immortal salvation of his children were at stake, have been so careless of his speech? Would he have chosen language so liable to be mistaken? Would he not rather have announced the awful truth in words which would admit of no possible doubt? Beside, if the terrors of this punishment are so effectual in preventing transgression, this was an-other reason for a specific declaration of the consequences of disobedience. If the argument on this point is good, a plain, open threat of endless woe at the very gate of Eden, as they entered, might have kept them back from the forbidden tree, and saved them and our race from the dreadful evils which followed the introduction of sin into the world.

But let us now turn to the record of their transgression, and of some other examples, where, if the doctrine is of divine origin and authority, we may surely expect to find it announced, and the weight of its awful curse brought down upon the guilty victims.

1. *The first transgression.* Gen. iiI 1-16. As this is the beginning of the sor-rowful tragedy of evil, we may look for some distinct revelation of the doc-trine in review, if it is of God; yet not one word is said in reference to it, nor is there any threat of punishment that can be mistaken for it!

The serpent is cursed, and the ground is cursed; but neither the man nor the woman! And observe carefully all the words of the sentence, and while mention is made of evils to be endured in this life, not the most distant allu-sion is made to any evil or punishment beyond this life. Now, if the doctrine of interminable torment after death be true, how are we to account for this? Can it be possible that God would be so careful to mention all the lesser evils, and wholly omit all mention of the terrible woes that are to have no end?

Who can believe that a just lawgiver and ruler would deal thus with his people? And of all things who can believe that the divine Father would deal thus treacherously with His own children?

But how differently the case stands, when we come to the doctrine of a present retribution for sin. In the very outset God warns our first parents against transgression, and in the most positive terms declares to Adam, "*In the day* thou eatest thereof *thou shalt surely die.*" Is not this clear enough? In

8

the very day of transgression they should die, or suffer the punishment of their sin, and this *surely,* beyond question or doubt. And was this assurance of God fulfilled? Most certainly; for they had no sooner sinned, than the retribution began, and they died to the peace and joy of innocence. The day of transgression was the day of judgment. They found that the wages of sin were death, or, in other words, misery, fear, anguish, and all the direful consequences of wrong. And that their case may profit their posterity, a careful statement of the mournful consequences of the transgression is made up, and put on record as a warning to future generations.

2. *Cain; or the murder of Abel.* Gen. iV 1-16. Here we have an example of the greatest of all crimes, *murder* - the murder of a brother! Surely we may now expect the doctrine of endless punishment to be revealed; and it would seem that, if true, there is no possible way to avoid mention of it. This was the first instance of this awful crime, and, Cain standing exposed to the fearful penalty, this was the time to roll the thunder of its terrors through the world, as a warning to all coming generations! This *must* have been done, if true; and yet in the whole account we have not a single word on the subject, not the slightest intimation that any such punishment was threatened.

The whole record is as follows: "And the Lord said unto Cain, The voice of thy brother's blood crieth unto me from the ground! And now art thou cursed from the earth, which hath opened her mouth to receive thy brother's blood from thy hand. When thou tillest the ground, it shall not henceforth yield unto thee her strength; a fugitive and a vagabond shalt thou be in the earth."

This is all we have in the way of punishment or threatenings; and is there anything here that looks like endless torments beyond this life? anything that would suggest the idea of such a judgment? Nothing at all; the guilty man is cursed from the earth, which is to refuse her fruits to his culture, and is driven out a vagabond; and there is the end of the account.

And it is evident that Cain did not understand the threats of judgment as implying endless woe, for his fears are all confined to the earth - the dread of revenge, of being killed, and the horrors of the life of an outcast and a vagabond. "And Cain said unto the Lord, My punishment is greater than I can bear. Behold, thou hast driven me out this day from the face of the earth; and from thy face shall I be hid; and I shall be a fugitive and a vagabond in the earth; and it shall come to pass that every one who findeth me shall slay me." These are all the evils of which Cain makes mention; and in view of them he exclaims, "My punishment is greater than I can bear."

Now, we put the question, can it be that, beside the punishments here named, Cain was to be subjected to endless torments after death, and yet be left wholly ignorant of the dreadful fate that awaited him? And if the guilty and wretched man thought the punishment actually denounced greater than he could bear, what would he have said, if, in addition to this, there had been threatened the agonies of an endless hell?

And is it possible to believe, if this was the purpose of God, that He would be wholly silent in regard to it? Was it *right* to be silent, if the terrible fate of Cain could have served as a warning and a restraint to all who should come after him?

In verse 15, "Therefore, whosoever slayeth Cain, vengeance shall be taken on him seven-fold." If infinite, endless torment is the punishment of Cain, how can *seven-fold more than this* be inflicted on another? Yet so it is written, and, therefore, either Cain's punishment was not endless woe, or there can be such a thing as *seven-fold endless woe!*

3. The deluge, or the destruction of the old world. Gen. vi – viii. Here we have one of the most remarkable examples of wickedness and judgment recorded in the Bible; and if ever anything is to be said on the subject of endless punishment, we may look for it here with the certainty of finding it. The description of the exceeding wickedness of the people who were destroyed in the flood may be seen in verses 5, 11, and 13, of chapter vi. The heart was given to evil, and "only evil continually;" "the earth was filled with violence, and all flesh had corrupted his way upon the earth." Here, then, was precisely the time, here the circumstances, which required the revelation and preaching of endless punishment, if, as affirmed, its influence is retaining and saving. This was the occasion, of all others, to make it known, that, through its terrifying and subduing power, the depraved and corrupted people might be turned from their sins, and the world thereby saved from the overwhelming horrors of the flood.

And yet here, too, not one word is said on the subject in the whole account. Noah, who was "a preacher of righteousness," was not a preacher of endless punishment. No mention is made of his ever having breathed a syllable in reference to it; nor is there a single line in the record of this event, showing that God threatened this, or that any attempt was made to restrain or reform the people through its influence. If the doctrine exerts the favorable influence ascribed to it, did God do all He *might* have done to reform and save them?

But again; in the account of their judgment we are told that they were destroyed by the flood from the face of the earth, everything that had breath; and with this the record closes. - vi 11-17; vii 10-24. Now if, as asserted, they were not only destroyed by the flood, but were afterwards subjected to the tortures of the world of ceaseless woe, is it not passing strange that no mention is made of this - not even an allusion to it? Is it possible that everything else should be carefully related, even to the height of the waters above the mountains, and the number of days they prevailed, and yet that the endless and indescribable torments of hell, the most terrible part of the judgment, and the most important to the world and to us, should be wholly omitted, and that without one word of explanation?

4. Destruction of Sodom and Gomorrah. Gen. xviiI, xix. Here we have another instance of remarkable wickedness, and of terrible judgment. Yet, on examination, we find no warning given to the Sodomites of an endless fire, to which the soul would be subjected, after the fire by which the body should

perish. The extreme wickedness of the people is set forth with graphic power, in the scene described in chapter xviiI 23-33; and it would seem a proper occasion for a revelation of endless punishment, if true; for such, if any, must certainly be its victims. But if we turn to the record, chapter xix. 24, 25, we find it contains no hint of the matter, neither in the way of warning to the Sodomites, nor of history for restraining future transgressors. If true, how is this omission to be explained in harmony with the acknowledged principles of justice, to say nothing of mercy?

What would we say of a ruler who should publish a law, affixing to it the penalty of ten stripes forevery transgression; and then, having inflicted this, should proceed to burn the offender over a slow fire, till he sank under the torture and died? And what should we think, if, with devilish ingenuity, he should contrive to keep every one of his victims alive for a whole year, for ten years, in order that the slow torture might be lengthened out that time; and all this kept secret when the law was published, and the trivial penalty of ten stripes declared as *the* punishment?

Yet this is precisely the state of the case in the judgment under review, if the Sodomites were sent into endless torments.

The difficulty is not removed by reference to Jude 7. For, in the first place, the expression, "suffering the vengeance of eternal fire," does not establish the point of endless suffering, - "eternal" fire and *endless* fire being two things, quite distinct from each other. The original word means simply indefinite time. In the second place, it is said, they are "set forth as an EXAMPLE, suffering the vengeance," &c. Now the very argument is based on the fact, that the history of the overthrow of Sodom does *not* furnish an example of endless torment, since not one word is said on the subject by Moses, from beginning to end of his account! Where, then, is the *example?*

Admitting the common interpretation of Jude to be correct, it is involved in inextricable difficulty; for, 1st. It states a falsehood, since the Sodomites were *not* set forth as an *example* of endless punishment in the invisible world, as no record of it is given by Moses, or the prophets, or any sacred writer. 2d. How is it that all mention of the matter should have been omitted until the time of Jude, and then be introduced, as it clearly is, incidentally, in the way of illustration? If there is any restraining power in the example, why was it concealed from the world more than two thousand years? Why was not the awful fate which awaited them revealed to the victims in the first place? It might have saved them. Why did not the sacred historian give account of it, that the millions who lived and perished between the event and the time of Jude, might have had the benefit of the example? If he was inspired, did he not know it? and if so, why was he silent?

But, as an example of divine judgment on the wicked here, in this world, visible to all future generations of men, the destruction of Sodom was worthy of special note, and exactly to the point of Jude's argument. And it is under this light that it is seen by some of the best-informed orthodox commentators.

Benson, in his note on the place, says: "By their *suffering the punishment of eternal fire,* St. Jude did not mean that those wicked persons were then, and would be always, burning in hell-fire. For he intimates that what they suffered was set forth to *public view,* and appeared to all as an example, or specimen, of God's displeasure against vice. That fire which consumed Sodom, &c., might be called *eternal,* as it burned till it had utterly consumed them, beyond the possibility of their ever being inhabited, or rebuilt."

Whitby's remarks are similar: "They are said to suffer the vengeance of eternal fire, not because their souls are at present punished in hell-fire, but because they, and their cities, perished by that fire from heaven, which brought a perpetual and irreparable destruction on them... Nor is there anything more common and familiar in Scripture, than to represent a thorough and irreparable visitation, whose effects and signs should be still remaining, by the word *aionios,* which we here render *eternal.*"

Gilpin says: "The apostle cannot well mean *future punishments,* because he mentions it as something that was to be a *visible example* to all." And others to the same effect: - see Paige's Selections on the place.

And thus we might follow out the inquiry in regard to every case of exceeding wickedness, or of great crimes; and we should find a specific statement, in every case, of the judgments inflicted on earth, up to the article of death, but the same marvelous silence in regard to the additional judgment of endless torment after death. We have accounts of the Builders of Babel, Joseph's Brethren, the Destruction of Pharaoh and his Host, Lot's Wife, &c., but not a word in any of these of any judgment kindred to endless woe - not a word of any judgment after death. If these sinners were given over, after suffering the punishments recorded in the Bible, to infinitely greater punishments to be perpetuated without end, then the most studied concealment has been purposely maintained in regard to the subject by the Scripture writers, or else they were as utterly ignorant of the whole matter as we are.

But no conceivable reason can be imagined for concealing this tremendous fact, if it were a fact, but every reason for revealing and affirming it to all the world. If they had known or believed anything of the sort, they could not have been silent. The only possible inference is, that the people before the Law certainly knew nothing about the doctrine of endless torments after death. If true, it had not been revealed in the long period of two thousand five hundred years, from the creation to the giving of the Law on Mount Sinal It is impossible to believe that, if true, God would have kept His children in the dark all this while; that no hint of it, no allusion to it, should have found place in His revelation to the Patriarchs; that He should never have threatened anything bordering upon it, in such cases of extreme wickedness as that of Cain, the Sodomites, and the corrupt inhabitants of the old world.

The just and inevitable conclusion then, is, that for twenty-five centuries, God had no design or thought of inflicting so dreadful an evil as endless punishment on His children. And, therefore, if we find it revealed in any subsequent portion of the Bible, it will be evident that it is a purpose which He has

12

formed since the Patriarchal period; that it was not a part of His original plan of the world, but something which He has incorporated into it since.

The next step, therefore, in this inquiry, is to make examination of the Law records, in order to ascertain if we have any revelation of the doctrine there.

Chapter Two - The Period Under the Law

It is now quite extensively known and allowed, by believers in the doctrine of endless punishment, that it is not revealed nor recognized by the Law of Moses. The facts in this regard are so palpable and conclusive to every diligent student of the Bible, that it would be difficult to deny that the Mosaic dispensation is altogether a dispensation of earthly rewards and punishments; that its retributions follow promptly on the steps of transgression. Both the records of the Law, and the history of the Jewish people through a period of fifteen hundred years, show this with a distinctness and fullness beyond all question, as we shall presently see.

Section I. Argument from The Law Itself, and from The History of the Jews

Let us first examine the remarkable statement of the question contained in Deuteronomy xxviii Space will allow me to quote only a few verses, but I earnestly solicit the reader, before going any further, to take up the Bible and carefully peruse the entire chapter, which is exceedingly important to our inquiry.

"It shall come to pass, if thou wilt not hearken unto the voice of the Lord thy God, to observe to do all His commandments and statutes which I command thee this day, that all these curses shall come upon thee, and overtake thee: Cursed shalt thou be in the city, and cursed shalt thou be in the field. Cursed shall be thy basket and thy store. Cursed shall be the fruit of thy body, and the fruit of thy land, the increase of thy cattle, and the flocks of thy sheep. Cursed shalt thou be when thou comest in, and cursed shalt thou be when thou goest out. The Lord shall send upon thee cursing, vexation and rebuke in all that thou settest thine hand unto for to do... He shall smite thee with consumption, and with a fever, with blasting and mildew; and the Lord shall make the pestilence cleave unto thee, until he shall have consumed thee from off the land whither thou goest to possess it.

"Moreover, all these curses shall come upon thee, and shall pursue thee till thou be destroyed; because thou hearkenedst not unto the voice of the Lord thy God, to keep his commandments and his statutes, which he commanded thee. Because thou servedst not the Lord thy God with joyfulness, and with gladness of heart, for the abundance of all things, therefore shalt thou serve thine enemies which the Lord shall send against thee, in hunger, and in thirst, and in nakedness, and in want of all things. And thine enemy shall besiege thee in all thy gates, until thy high and fenced walls come down, wherein thou trustedst. Thou shalt beget sons and daughters, but thou shalt not enjoy them; for they shall go into captivity. And thou shalt become an astonishment, a proverb, and a byword, among all nations whither the Lord shall lead thee."

Now here, in this important document, we have set out at great length, and with every variety of specification, the judgments and punishments with which God threatens to visit the Jews for their transgressions of His laws; but not a word is uttered in respect to the punishments of an endless hell after death. All the evils which are to fall upon them are of a temporal character, such only as can be inflicted on them while in the body, while on the earth: plagues and sickness, murrain on the cattle, and mildew on their vines and grains; locusts in the fields and orchards; hunger, thirst, and nakedness; curses on the city and country, curses at home and abroad; the desolation of their country by their enemies, exile and captivity.

These are the only penalties annexed to the Law of Moses of which we have any information; and these were fully visited on the heads of the offending and rebellious people. "There runs through their history a system of strict and retributive judgment, whereof the God of Jacob is the administrator. Within the pale of this peculiar dispensation, virtue met its recompense, and vice its punishment, with a regularity that was at once unfailing and notorious. The nation is presented to us under very different attitudes; under judges, under kings, in peace and in war, victorious and vanquished, prosperous and afflicted, at home and abroad, free and in bondage; but whatever the situation or period in which we view their history, we are met at once by the principle in question."

This is strictly true. The entire history of the Jewish people as a nation, and as individuals, from generation to generation, shows with what exactness the threatenings of the law were fulfilled in judgments. When they were obedient, the Lord prospered them, and rewarded them with fruitful seasons, with increasing wealth and power, and made them superior to their enemies. But when they were rebellious and wicked, then followed adversity, defeat, captivity, and all the physical calamities threatened in the Law.

But all this while we have not one syllable of an endless woe which is to be added to all the other woes. In no instance of rebellion against God, not when their corruption and idolatry were at the highest reach of crime and blasphemy, do we find them threatened with the torments of a hell beyond the present life.

Now, if they really were exposed to this, if they have been actually cast into this hell, it is the most unaccountable thing, in the government of God, that He should do this without one note of warning to the victims; and at the same time leave not a line or a word of their awful fate on record, as a terror to future transgressors!

14

But let us now look at one or two cases of individual crime, where we may justly expect to find some open declaration of the doctrine, if true.

1. *The case of Abimelech.* Judges ix.

We have his offense stated in verses 5 and 6: "And Abimelech went unto his father's house at Ophrah, and slew his brethren, the sons of Jerubbaal, being three score and ten persons, upon one stone... And all the men of Shechem gathered together at the house of Millo, and went and made Abimelech king."

Here is the sin, and it is horrible enough. Nothing can surpass this bloody sacrifice on the altar of ambition. At one fell stroke seventy murders, save one, and the victims his own brethren, bone of his bone, flesh of his flesh; and through this sea of kindred blood, he waded to the throne! Surely, if ever there was a sinner of the hue of "the blackness of darkness," this Abimelech was the man; and if the flaming pit of endless woe is not a fiction, but a solemn fact, we shall now hear something of it in the way of recompensing the sin of this guilty wretch.

Well, here is the record: "And Abimelech came unto the tower and fought against it, and a certain woman cast a piece of millstone upon Abimelech's head, and all to break his skull. Then he called hastily to the young man, his armor-bearer, and said unto him, Draw thy sword and slay me, that men say not of me, a woman slew him. And his young man thrust him through, and he died... Thus God rendered the wickedness of Abimelech, which he did unto his father, in slaying his seventy brethren: and all the evil of the men of Shechem did God render upon their heads." Verses 52-57; also 46-49.

This is the whole record of judgment; but, as we see, not a word of endless punishment. The cruel and bloody man is followed with evil, with rebellion from his former friends, who made him king; and at last, after many struggles, he is slain in battle, and the men of Shechem are burned alive in their strongholds. And there the account ends, with only this brief statement: "*Thus* God rendered the wickedness of Abimelech," &c. Of course if it was *thus,* or in the way set forth, then it cannot be that he is to be recompensed by endless woe. The recompense is complete, is a past event of earth, and cannot therefore be in a future world, perpetuated through eternity.

And of the men of Shechem it is affirmed, that God rendered upon their heads *"all the evil"* they had done. Past time again - then and there He recompensed them; and not for a part, but for *all* their evil doings. In the words of Bishop Patrick, "God, the Judge of all, punished Abimelech and the men of Shechem according to their deserts, and made them the instruments of each other's destruction; and it is remarkable that this punishment overtook them speedily, within less than four years after their crime was committed."

As yet, then, we have no revelation of the doctrine in review, but only the infliction of the temporal punishments of the Law. But one more example, of another sort.

2. *Ahithophel, the Suicide.* 2 Sam. xvii

In the wickedness and death of this man we have a case of great moment. He was a very bad, unprincipled and cruel man; and, as Dr. Clarke says, *"died an unprepared and accursed death."* He laid violent hands on himself, and this too in the midst of his wickedness! Of such persons, the reader well knows what is said by believers in endless punishment: "There is no hope for them - they die in sin, without repentance - their very last act is a crime, for which there can be no punishment in this life - there is no change after death; therefore they must sink into the endless torments of hell."

This being the case, then, we shall surely hear of it now. If true, and we are to have any revelation of it under the Law, we have come at last to the very occasion which will call it out. The doom of the guilty suicide will be clearly and distinctly announced as a warning to all who shall attempt to follow in his steps. Let us then turn to the record:

"And when Ahithophel saw that his counsel was not followed, he saddled his ass, and arose and gat him home to his house, to his city, and put his household in order, *and hanged himself, and died, and was buried in the sepulcher of his father."* vs. 23.

This is all - every word! Not a syllable of his being sent to a place of perpetual torture after his death. We are told that he hanged himself, died, and was buried; and there the sacred historian leaves him, without one word of comment. Now, if there ever lived a man likely to come into the pit of torments, if there be such a place, this wicked suicide was the man; and is it a supposable case that, such being his doom, the divine writer would or could have passed it over in silence?

Would he be careful to mention the unimportant matters, that he saddled his ass, put his household in order, was buried in his father's sepulcher, &c., and yet not utter *so much as one word* in regard to the awful subject of the interminable torments beyond the burial and the grave? Who can believe this without an accusation against the justice and mercy of God toward all coming generations?

So far, then, the Law itself in its statement of penalties, the history of the nation of the Jews, and of the most remarkable cases of crime under the Law, preserve a profound silence on the subject in hand. Not a word, not the most obscure allusion to the doctrine of unending punishment, is to be met with in any of the divine records of transgressions or judgments.

Section II. The Testimony of Orthodox Critics and Theologians

The purpose of this section is to confirm the argument of the preceding section by calling in as witnesses some of the most learned and impartial scholars and divines of the Orthodox school, themselves believers in the dogma of an endless hell, but confessing that it is not taught in the Law of Moses, nor in the Old Testament.

1. MILMAN. "The sanction on which the Hebrew Law was founded is extraordinary. The lawgiver (Moses) maintains a profound silence on that fundamental article, if not of political, at least of religious legislation - rewards and punishments in another life. He substituted temporal chastisements and temporal blessings. On the violation of the constitution followed inevitably blighted harvests, famine, pestilence, defeat, captivity; on its maintenance, abundance, health, fruitfulness, victory, independence. How wonderfully the event verified the prediction of the inspired legislator! how invariably apostasy led to adversity - repentance and reformation to prosperity!"

2. BISHOP WARBURTON. "In the Jewish Republic, both the rewards and punishments promised by Heaven were temporal only. Such as health, long life, peace, plenty, and dominion, &c. Diseases, premature death, war, famine, want, subjections, and captivity, &c. And in no one place of the Mosaic Institutes is there the least mention, or any intelligible hint, of the rewards and punishments of another life.

"When Solomon restored the integrity of religion, he addressed a long prayer to the God of Israel, consisting of one solemn petition for the continuance of the *old covenant,* made by the ministry of Moses. He gives an exact account of all its parts, and explains at large the sanctions of the Jewish Law and Religion. And here, as in the writings of Moses, we find nothing but *temporal rewards and punishments.*"

Warburton, and also Whateley, quoted below, take ground that the doctrine of a future existence is not recognized in the Old Testament. In this they are wrong, as we have attempted to show in the fifth section of this chapter.

3. ARNAULD. This author is quoted by Warburton, who calls him "a great and shining ornament of the Gallican (Catholic) church." His testimony is the following: "It is the height of ignorance to doubt this truth, which is one of the most common of the Christian Religion, and *which is attested by all the Fathers,* that the promises of the Old Testament were temporal and earthly, and that the Jews worshipped God only for earthly blessings (les biens charnels)."

4. PALEY. "This (Mosaic) dispensation dealt in temporal rewards and punishments. In the 28th of Deuteronomy you find Moses, with prodigious solemnity, pronouncing the blessings and cursings which awaited the children of Israel under the dispensation to which they were called. And you will observe, that these blessings consisted *altogether* of worldly benefits, and these curses of worldly punishments."

5. PROF. WINES. "It is conceded that Moses did not annex to his laws the promised joys and threatened terrors of eternity...The Hebrew legislator was restrained from annexing future punishments as sanctions to his laws, by considerations arising out of the character of his mission, &c."

6. JAHN, whose excellent work is a text-book in Andover Theological Seminary, says: "We have not authority, therefore, decidedly to say, that any other motives were held out to the ancient Hebrews to pursue good and avoid evil,

than those which were derived from the rewards and punishments of this life."

7. PROF. MAYER, late of the Theological Seminary of the Reformed Dutch Church, in Pennsylvania, has the following in a recent volume of Sermons: "It is evident to the careful reader that, both in the book of Job and in the Pentateuch, the divine judgment which is spoken of is always a judgment that takes place in this life; and the rewards which are promised to the righteous, and the punishments that are threatened to the wicked, are such only as are awarded in the present state of being...No mention is anywhere made, in the writings of Moses, of a judgment at the end of this world. The idea that God is the judge of the world, pervades them everywhere; but it has always relation to this earthly existence."

8. ARCHBISHOP WHATELEY. After a lengthy argument on the subject, he says: "Is not, then, the conclusion inevitable, that, if the doctrine of future retribution had been to be revealed, or any traditional knowledge of it confirmed, we should have found it explicitly stated, and still more frequently repeated than the temporal sanctions of the Law? And when, instead of anything like this, we have set before us a few scattered texts, which, it is contended, allude to, or imply, this doctrine, can it be necessary to examine whether they are rightly interpreted? Surely it is a sufficient reply, to say that, if Moses had intended to inculcate such doctrine, he would have clearly stated and dwelt on it in almost every page. Nor is it easy to conceive how any man of even ordinary intelligence, and not blinded by devoted attachment to an hypothesis, can attentively peruse the books of the Law, abounding as they do with such copious descriptions of the temporal rewards and punishments which sanction that Law, and with such earnest admonitions grounded on that sanction, and yet can bring himself seriously to believe that the doctrine of a state of retribution after death, which it cannot be contended is even mentioned, however slightly, in more than a very few passages, formed a part of the Mosaic revelation." [1]

Such is the testimony of these learned men, all of them believers in the doctrine of future endless punishment, but compelled by their superior knowledge to confess that the doctrine is not revealed, or alluded to by Moses, nor in any way made the motive of obedience to the laws he promulgated as the servant of God. Nothing but the strongest array of facts, nothing but the utter impossibility of finding any trace of it in the institutes of the old dispensation, could have induced these men to take a position so fatal to the truth of this doctrine; to make acknowledgements which render it forever impossible to establish the doctrine in harmony with divine justice and honor.

But the statements of these men, and the truth of our argument, are both confirmed by still higher authority. In his epistle to the Hebrews, Paul himself gives this positive and final testimony to the point, viz., that under the Law, "*every transgression and disobedience* RECEIVED a *just recompense of reward.*" ii 2.

18

This ought to settle the question forever; for, if every transgression actually received its just punishment, then endless punishment cannot be true; or, if true, this statement is a grand mistake, or a deliberate misrepresentation.

I really do not see any way of avoiding the decisive force of this open and unequivocal passage. The apostle certainly knew what he was writing, and could not have made any mistake in the expression of his thoughts. If, then, the words mean what they express, - if the text is a true statement of facts, and every transgression did actually receive a just recompense or retribution, - how is it possible to affirm that any one of these transgressions will be punished over again with endless torments, without charging God with the most monstrous injustice and cruelty?

It seems as if no honest mind, no sincere believer in the authority of God's word, could appeal from a testimony so positive and unmistakable as this. There is no room for comment or criticism. In the presence of such an unimpeachable witness, the question is reduced to its simplest form: either to abandon the Bible argument, or to abandon the doctrine of endless punishment.

But we would not silence by mere authority, but convince. The statement of the apostle is supported and illustrated by the whole course of Bible history; and fix on what offense you will, be it national or individual, be it offense of priest, king, prophet, or peasant, and it will be found that every instance of disobedience was promptly met with its just recompense. And it is a most instructive and morally profitable study to follow the traces of this present retribution, as they appear in the Old Testament; and with this view I give the following condensed summary, taken from a work entitled, "A System of Temporal Retribution indicated from Scripture and Observation;" written singularly enough, and with marvelous inconsistency, by a Presbyterian minister, believing in a *future* retribution:

"The chosen people, in their passage through the wilderness, sinned frequently and provoked their God to anger. They are punished by hunger and thirst, fire belched forth from the bowels of the earth, and consumed some of the offenders, a plague came down upon them, fiery serpents invaded their camp, and stung great numbers of the people, their journey was drawn out into a weary wandering for forty years in a barren desert, and finally there were but two of that whole generation who were suffered to enter into the land of promise. Moses and Aaron, the two leaders of the host, although faithful in the main, yet having sinned, the one by anger, and the other by countenancing the people in their idolatry, are not permitted to set foot on Canaan. The sons of Eli disgrace the office of the priesthood by their unholy acts; a sentence from on high is pronounced against them, and they are slain as they bore the ark in battle with the Philistines. Balaam contends against Israel in spite of God's command to the contrary, and in return for his frowardness is killed in battle. The whole career of Saul bears testimony to a system of temporal retribution. Throughout his reign he was guilty of continual declensions from the law of that God who had given him the scepter, and accordingly he was visited with frequent reverses; his unchecked passions distempered his mind, and subjected him to seasons of madness and frenzy; his life is poisoned with jealousy, fear and remorse, and at length, when he had refused reproof and persisted in sin, he dies by his own hand on the field of battle. David, the man after God's own heart, is guilty of the heavy offenses of adultery and murder; he is *expressly* punished by the death of the child, and there was a series of misfortunes from this time to the close of his reign, which were sent as further chastisements of his dark crimes. Joab is guilty of deeds of wanton violence and bloodshed. Prosperity attends him throughout the reign of David, but under Solomon his sin finds him out, and he who had 'shed the blood of war in peace' is in his turn slain by the sword. Solomon carries too far the indulgence given the Jewish monarchs of a plurality of wives. His wisdom raised him above their evil influence during the vigor of his life, but in his declining years his wives become a snare to him, seduce him to adopt their idolatrous practices, and leave it a matter of considerable doubt whether the wise king really died in the faith of his fathers. Jeroboam encouraged his people in the worship of idols, and, in consequence, the favor of the Lord departed from him and his household and kingdom. Ahab and Jezebel favored the false prophets, insulted the prophets of the Lord, practiced oppression, fraud and cruelty, and they are notably punished for their dark offenses; the one is slain in battle, the other is cast from her window and devoured by the dogs. The princes and the people in general having through many generations grievously departed from the law of the Lord, they are carried into captivity in Babylon, where during seventy years they endure all the bitter evils of exile, bondage and oppression. Nebuchadnezzar insults the majesty of heaven by his pride, ambition, and ungodliness. He is cast down from his high place, and he who aspired to be equal with Jehovah is debased below the condition of the meanest among men, being doomed during seven years to herd with the beasts of the field, to feed with them on the same fare, and to repair with them to the same caverns. Belshazzar, forgetful of the warnings and the judgments that befell his grandsire, exhibits the same overweening arrogance, conjoined with profligacy and profanity. Vengeance descends upon him in the hour of his loftiest pride and exaltation. As he sat in the midst of his nobles and captains, rioting in drunkenness, sacrilege and licentiousness, a spectral hand is seen by him to write his doom in mystical characters on the wall, the sentence is expounded to him by the prophet of the Lord, and that very night his city was taken and sacked, he himself was slain, and his kingdom was given to another. Haman cherishes a deadly jealousy against the upright Mordecai, and carries his hatred so far as to erect a gallows on which he proposes to hang the object of his enmity. His dark schemes are discovered and turned against himself, and he and his sons are hanged on the gibbet which he had prepared for another."

Thus we see how perfectly the facts illustrate the declaration of the apostle, that under the law "every transgression and disobedience *received* a just recompense of reward." This of necessity excludes the idea of a future endless retribution; as well as the important fact, already named, that through all this long and various record of sin and its punishments, no mention is made, nor the least intelligible hint given, of any such thing. We cannot, therefore, suppose it to be true, without a most extraordinary violation, on the part of God, of every principle of honor, justice, and mercy.

Section III. Argument from the Word "Sheol," Or the Old Testament Doctrine of Hell.

The word Hell, in the Old Testament, is always a translation of the Hebrew word *Sheol,* which occurs sixty-four times, and is rendered "hell" thirty-two times, "grave" twenty-nine times, and "pit" three times.

1. By examination of the Hebrew Scriptures it will be found that its radical or primary meaning is, *The place or state of the dead.*

The following are examples: "Ye shall bring down my gray hairs with sorrow to the grave." Gen. xvii 38. "I will go down to the grave to my son mourning." xxxviii 35. "O that thou wouldst hide me in the grave!" Job xiV 13. "My life draweth nigh to the grave." Ps. lxxxviii 3. "In the grave who shall give thee thanks?" lxxxvi 5. "Our bones are scattered at the grave's mouth." cxlI 7. "There is no work, nor device, nor knowledge, nor wisdom, in the grave, whither thou goest." Ecc. ix. 10. "If I ascend up into heaven, thou art there: if I make my bed in hell, behold thou art there." Ps. cxxxix. 8. "Hell from beneath is moved to meet thee, at thy coming. It stirreth up the dead for thee," &c. Isaiah xiv. 9-15.

These passages show the Hebrew usage of the word *sheol,* which is the original of the word "grave" and "hell" in all the examples cited. It is plain that it has here no reference to a place of endless torment after death. The patriarch would scarcely say, "I will go down to an endless hell to my son mourning." He did not believe his son was in any such place. Job would not very likely pray to God to hide him in a place of endless torment, in order to be delivered from his troubles.

If the reader will substitute the word "hell" in the place of "grave" in all these passages, he will be in the way of understanding the Scripture doctrine on this subject.

2. But there is also a figurative sense to the word *sheol,* which is frequently met with in the later Scriptures of the Old Testament. Used in this sense, it represents *a state of degradation or calamity, arising from any cause, whether misfortune, sin, or the judgment of God.*

This is an easy and natural transition. The state or the place of the dead was regarded as solemn and gloomy, and thence the word sheol, the name of this place, came to be applied to any gloomy, or miserable state or condition. The following passages are examples: "The sorrows of hell compassed me about; the snares of death prevented me." Psalm xvii 4-6. This was a past event, and therefore the hell must have been this side of death. Solomon, speaking of a child, says, "Thou shalt beat him, and deliver his soul from hell;" that is, from the ruin and woe of disobedience. ProV xxiI 14. The Lord says to Israel, in reference to their idolatries, "Thou didst debase thyself even unto hell." Isaiah lvii 9. This, of course, signifies a state of utter moral degradation and wickedness, since the Jewish nation as such certainly never went down into a hell of ceaseless woe. Jonah says, "Out of the belly of hell cried I, and thou heardst me." ii 2. Here we see the absurdity of supposing *sheol* or *hell* to mean a place of punishment after death. The hell in this case was the belly of the whale; or rather the wretched and suffering condition in which the disobedient prophet found himself. "The pains of hell got hold on me: I found trouble and sorrow." Ps. cxvi 3. Yet David was a living man, all this while, here on the earth. So he exclaims again, "Great is thy mercy towards me. Thou hast delivered my soul from the lowest hell." Ps. lxxxvi 13. Now here the Psalmist was in the lowest hell, and was delivered from it, while he was yet in the body, *before* death. Of course the hell here cannot be a place of endless punishment *after* death.

These passages sufficiently illustrate the figurative usage of the word *sheol*, "hell." They show plainly that it was employed by the Jews as a symbol or figure of extreme degradation or suffering, without reference to the cause. And it is to this condition the Psalmist refers when he says, "The wicked shall be turned into hell, and all the nations that forget God." Ps. ix. 17. Though Dr. Allen, President of Bowdoin College, thinks "the punishment expressed here is cutting off from life, destroying from earth by some special judgment, and removing to the invisible place of the dead" *(sheol).*

It is plain, then, from these citations, that the word *sheol*, "hell," makes nothing for the doctrine of future unending punishment as a part of the Law penalties. It is never used by Moses or the Prophets in the sense of a place of torment after death; and in no way conflicts with the statement already proved, that the Law of Moses deals wholly in temporal rewards and punishments.

This position, also, I wish to fortify by the testimony of Orthodox critics, men of learning and candor. They know, and therefore they speak.

1. CHAPMAN. "Sheol, in itself considered, has no connection with future punishment." *Cited by Balfour, First Inquiry.*

2. DR. ALLEN, quoted above, says: "The term *sheol* does not seem to mean, with certainty, anything more than the state of the dead in their deep abode."

3. DR. CAMPBELL. "Sheol signifies the state of the dead without regard to their happiness or misery."

4. DR. WHITBY. "Sheol throughout the Old Testament signifies not the place of punishment, or of the souls of bad men only, but the grave only, or the place of death."

5. DR. MUENSCHER. This distinguished author of a Dogmatic History in German, says: "The souls or shades of the dead wander in *sheol*, the realm or kingdom of death, an abode deep under the earth. Thither go all men, without distinction, and hope for no return. There ceases all pain and anguish;

there reigns an unbroken silence; there all is powerless and still; and even the praise of God is heard no more."

6. VON COELLN. "*Sheol* itself is described as the house appointed for all living, which receives into its bosom all mankind, without distinction of rank, wealth, or moral character. It is only in the mode of death, and not in the condition after death, that the good are distinguished above the evil. The just, for instance, die in peace, and are gently borne away before the evil comes; while a bitter death breaks the wicked like as a tree." [2]

These witnesses all testify that *sheol,* or *hell,* in the Old Testament, has no reference whatever to this doctrine; that it signifies simply the state of the dead, the invisible world, without regard to their goodness or badness, their happiness or misery. The Old Testament doctrine of hell, therefore, is not the doctrine of endless punishment. It is not revealed in the Law of Moses. It is not revealed in the Old Testament. To such result has our inquiry led us; and now what shall we say of it?

Section IV. The Moral Application of the Preceding Arguments

There is no doubt that Moses was acquainted with the doctrine of future endless punishments. It was the common doctrine of Egypt, as all agree; and "Moses was learned in all the wisdom of the Egyptians." Acts vii 22. And yet, knowing it as thoroughly as he must have done, he never alludes to it once in all his laws and penalties, but rejects it utterly from his doctrines and institutions. He will have nothing to do with it. He not only repudiates the gross fables and superstitions of the Egyptians in regard to the future world, but the entire substance of future punishments; and, by his studied silence, shows he has no faith in their truth or utility. [3]

Is it possible to imagine a more conclusive proof against the divine origin of the doctrine? If he had believed it to be of God, if he had believed in endless torments as the doom of the wicked after death, and had received this as a revelation from heaven, could he have passed it over in silence? Would he have dared to conceal it, or treat so terrible a subject with such marked contempt? And what motive could he have had for doing this?

I cannot conceive of a more striking evidence of the fact that the doctrine is not of God. He knew whence the monstrous dogma came, and He had seen enough of Egypt already, and would have no more of her cruel superstitions; and so He casts this out, with her abominable idolatries, as false and unclean things.

But, if the doctrine be true, there is another consideration of still greater moment. If it be true, and for four thousand years the wicked have been plunging into the flaming pit, how, as we have said, are we to clear the character of God from the charge of the most cruel indifference, the most monstrous injustice? What *can* be said in defense of such a course of proceeding?

Look at it. He resolves to inflict unutterable and endless tortures on His guilty children; He annexes this as a penalty to His law; He reveals the law, but He carefully conceals the awful penalty. His children know nothing at all of the terrible fate which awaits them; they are entirely ignorant of the tremendous fact that their transgressions of the law involve this dreadful result, this woe immortal and infinite, stretching into duration without end.

And God, their Father, sees them rushing on, year after year, age after age, and stumbling blindfolded down into the black gulf of death and torment, and yet speaks not one word of warning, gives not the slightest intimation to any of them that they are coming to such a doom! There He sits on the throne of the universe, with arms folded in the consciousness of power, with lips sealed in determined silence. He knows all, sees all; while His poor victims are walking in darkness, wholly ignorant of the frightful risk they are running, and of the deadly purpose of evil against them which their Maker has shut up in His own heart.

One word from Him might break the fatal spell; but that word is not spoken. His arm, stretched out for a moment, might turn back the rushing tide of ruin; but it remains motionless. No movement of His, no sound nor look, indicates the least interest in the shocking tragedy which is passing under His eye, and of which He is the author. For four thousand years He beholds this torrent of immortal souls pouring over the precipice of sin into the bottomless pit of damnation below; and through it all remains silent - never once speaks to them of their awful fate; nor seeks, by the terrors of it, to save the living from the doom of the dead!

What kind of a God is this? What claim has He to the name of Father? What kind of a Lawgiver is this, who publishes the law, but keeps the penalty concealed, a secret, with Himself only? What would be said of a king who should enact a code of laws, annexing to every one of them, as a warning to evildoers, the punishment of death; but never make this fact known to the people? And what if every transgressor were seized, and put to a most horrible death by torture, and this also kept secret from his friends and relations, and from all the world?

Yet this is precisely what God has done, as our argument shows, for four thousand years, if the doctrine of endless punishment be true! But even this is not the worst.

Suppose a parent, sending his child into a distant part of the country, should carefully specify every thorn-bush, and sharp stone, and difficult spot, along the road, and urge him to avoid them; but should with equal care conceal from him the fact that the road ended in a sheer precipice a thousand feet down into a fearful gulf of volcanic fire and flame - knowing at the same time that his son, if not warned, would certainly fall into this roaring crater and perish.

Yet this is exactly the course God has pursued with His children. He has carefully set out all the lesser penalties, as famine, disease, blasted fields and ruined flocks, defeat and captivity, as the punishments of their disobedience;

24

but He has as carefully concealed that greater judgment beyond all these, and in comparison with which all these a thousand fold increased are less than the dust in the balance.

Nay, in particular cases He even mentions the height of the waters, the going forth of a dove, the burning of a tower, a piece of millstone, the saddling of an ass, every smallest thing, but not a word of the great woe of woes!

I cannot help feeling, in view of this argument, how appropriate and forcible are the words of the author of the "Conflict of Ages:"

"God has made the human mind to have decided intuitive convictions as to what is consistent with equity and honor. These we are not violently to suppress by preconceived theories, or assumed facts. If any alleged actions of God come into collision with the natural and intuitive judgments of the human mind concerning what is honorable and right on the points specified, there is better reason to call in question the alleged facts, than to suppose those principles to be false which God has made the human mind intuitively to recognize as true. Moreover, we have divine authority for so doing; since, in a debate with the Jews, involving these points, God does not hesitate to appeal to these very principles, and to reason in perfect accordance with their common and obvious decisions. Ezek. xviii. 1-4, 19, 22, 25, 29, and xxxiiI 11, 17-20."

Nothing is truer than this. God has given us intuitive convictions as to what is consistent with equity and honor; and there never was a man on earth, however perverted or blinded by his creed, who could say, in his soul, that the conduct ascribed to God in the preceding argument, by the doctrine of endless punishment, is consistent with equity and honor. And this being the case, he has no right to say that God will do this thing; he has no right to attribute to his Father in heaven actions which any human parent would shrink from with horror and disgust.

But, if the doctrine be true, there is a darker feature yet in the case. Not only is God's word silent on this point, but it virtually denies it by asserting the opposite. Take the words of Paul, already quoted, that every transgression under the law has actually been justly recompensed. So David asserts that Jehovah "is a God that judgeth in the earth." Ps. Lviii. And by the prophet Jeremiah He says Himself, "I am the Lord, which exercise loving kindness, judgment and righteousness in the earth." Chap. ix. So again, "God judgeth the righteous, and God is angry with the wicked every day" - that is, every day He judges the righteous and the wicked, rewarding the one, and punishing the other. Ps. vii 11. Once more: Solomon says, "Behold, the righteous shall be recompensed in the earth; much more the wicked and the sinner." ProV xi 31.

Now these passages, part of a multitude, are in perfect chord with the Law, and declare a system of temporal rewards and punishments on the earth. Suppose future endless punishments after death to be true; then not only has God concealed the fact, but has done worse than this, by positively announcing that He exercises judgment in the earth, and that the righteous and the wicked are recompensed in the earth! Now, if endless punishment after death be true, these statements are false; but if these are true, then endless punishment is false. They cannot both be true; they cannot both be of God; for "it is impossible for God to lie." Heb. vi 18.

We are compelled, therefore, to look for the origin of this doctrine elsewhere than in the mind of God. One thing, at all events, is certain. No trace of it is found in the Old Testament, which is all the written record we have of the divine mind and purpose for the space of four thousand years. The Patriarchs knew nothing of it. Moses, who did know of it, having learned it in Egypt, repudiates it by his silence. The Law contains no vestige of it among all its penalties and threatenings. The Lamentations of Job, [4] the Psalms of David, the Proverbs of Solomon, the Predictions of the Prophets, make no mention of the horrible thing.

So far, then, the doctrine is not divine in its origin. It is not of that "wisdom from above," which "is first pure, then peaceable, gentle, easy to be entreated, full of mercy and good fruits, without partiality and without hypocrisy." But it must have come rather out of that wisdom which the apostle says is "earthly, sensual, devilish." James iiI 15-17.

Of course, if the doctrine was in existence during the Law period, if we find it among other nations, contemporary with the Jews, the conclusion is certain - since it was not of divine origin, it must have been of earthly origin; since it did not come from God, it must have had its source in the wisdom of this world, which is foolishness with God. To this point we shall direct our inquiries in the following chapter; but, before proceeding to this, we shall give attention, in the next section, to some objections which have been entered against the arguments of these first two chapters.

Section V. Objections Answered

In a review of the argument of the two preceding chapters, the following question has been proposed to the author: "Admitting that your argument drawn from the Old Testament sustains your position with regard to endless punishment, does it not apply with equal force against the doctrine of endless happiness? Does it not apply with equal force against all future existence, whatever?"

In replying to this, the last branch of the question legitimately comes first:

1. "Is not the argument equally good against any future existence whatever?"

No; for though the ideas of a future existence presented in the early Hebrew Scriptures are certainly very wide from those set forth in the Gospel, yet it would be equally wide of the truth to say they do not recognize any future life at all.

The very word *sheol* conveys the idea of existence, though it gives no intimation of the conditions or character of it. And in order to set out this point in clear light, which its great importance seems to demand, I shall quote at

26

some length from several distinguished Orthodox critics, whose testimony will help both to confirm the arguments already offered, and to answer the question in review.

PROF. STUART says: "*Sheol* designated the world of the dead, the region of *umbrae* or *ghosts*. It was considered as a vast and wide domain or region, of which the grave was only a part, or a kind of entrance-way. It appears to have been regarded as extending deep down into the earth, even to its lowest abysses. In this boundless region lived and moved, at times, the manes (or ghosts) of departed friends."

BISHOP LOWTH says: "In the under-world of the Hebrews there is something peculiarly grand and awful. It was an immense region, a vast subterranean kingdom, involved in thick darkness, filled with deep valleys, and shut up with strong gates; and from it there was no possibility of escape. Thither whole hosts of men went down at once; heroes and armies with their trophies of victory; kings and their people were found there, where they had a shadowy sort of existence as manes or ghosts, neither entirely spiritual, nor entirely material, engaged in the employments of their earthly life, though destitute of strength and physical substance."

HERDER says, among the early Hebrews "souls of the departed were regarded as powerless as shadows, without distinction of members, as a nerveless breath; having an animate though shadowy existence, they wandered and flitted in the realms of the dead, in the dark nether world, as limbless and powerless beings. Ghostly kings were seated upon shadowy thrones; kingdoms and states were there, and armies of the slain, but all was voiceless and still."

There is a perfect illustration of this in what is, perhaps, the finest poem in the Bible. Isaiah xiv. 3-23. It celebrates the downfall of the king of Babylon, and represents him as cast down to hell, *sheol,* or the under-world of spirits, and the former kings of the earth, whom he had destroyed, now inhabitants of that region, as exulting over him. I give a portion of the translation of Herder which the reader can compare with the common version:

"The ghostly realm beneath was roused for thee;
It moved to meet thee at thy coming;
It stirred up for thee the ghostly shades,
Even all the mighty ones of earth;
It raised them up from their thrones,
All the kings of the nations.
They all welcomed thee, and said,
Art thou also become a shadow like us?
Art thou, too, made even as we?
Brought down even to the dead is thy pride,
And low the triumphal sound of thy harps.
The couch beneath thee is the worm,
The mould of death thy covering.

27

How art thou fallen from heaven,
Bright star! thou son of the dawn!
How art thou crushed to the earth,
That didst conquer the nations!"

These testimonies are sufficient to show that the early Hebrews believed in a future existence, though their views of the world of the departed, and of their condition there, were very obscure. In the words of Dr. Barnes, "The apprehension seems to have been that all the dead would descend through the grave to a region where only a few scattered rays of light would exist, and where the whole aspect of the dwelling was in strong contrast with the cheerful region of the land of the living." "Even Job had not such cheerful anticipations of the future state as to cheer and support him in the time of trial." [5]

It is certain that the Hebrews had not such faith respecting the future existence of the soul, as those entertained by Christians of this day. God did not reveal all truth to them, and instruct them in that knowledge which constituted the fulness of the blessing of the Gospel of Christ. Had it been so, there would have been no occasion for the coming of the Saviour, for His death and resurrection, no room for the Christian revelation.

It was reserved for the Gospel to bring forth the great doctrine of the life immortal and ever-blessed in the fulness of its glory and worth. Dimly and imperfectly did the old patriarchs and their people see through the mists of death to the land beyond. The Law kindled no beacon fires in the shadowy valley, whose light revealed the country of the soul in all its beauty. This was the peculiar office of Christ and the Gospel, as Paul so distinctly affirms, when he speaks of the grace of God, "made manifest by the appearing of our Saviour Jesus Christ, who hath abolished death, and hath brought life and immortality to light (into light, or into the full light) through the Gospel." 2 Tim. I 8-10.

Of course, if this passage has any point or meaning, the doctrine of life and immortality was not *fully* revealed to the Jews, its conditions, and the character of its blessedness. The *fact* of a future life was made known to them; but the foregoing statements, based on the Old Testament Scriptures, show how far their views fell below the clear, spiritual doctrine of the Gospel.

As Prof. Bush observes, "The information couched in the Old Testament on this theme are comparatively dark and shadowy, more like the dim and feeble glimmerings of the morning twilight, than the unclouded blaze of the noon-day sun." In the same strain Prof. Stuart says, the

Hebrews "had not those distinct and definite notions on this subject, which we of the present day have. We should never forget that it is the glorious preeminence of the Gospel to have brought life and immortality to light. Christians too often forget this while reasoning from the Old Testament." Again he says: "I am far from coinciding with those who find the nature of a future world as fully and plainly revealed in the Old Testament as in the New.

But I am equally far from those who do not find it at all intimated there. Both these positions are extremes." [6]

This is a just statement of the case. The *nature* of the future existence is not set out, neither in the patriarchal, nor in the prophetical times of the old dispensation, as fully and as luminously as under the new dispensation of grace. But then it is absurd to say that there are no indications of this great truth in the Old Testament. When it is recorded that Abraham was "gathered to his people," we must understand something more than burial with his fathers or ancestors; for they were buried in Chaldea, and not in Canaan. Gen. xv 15, xxv 8. So Jacob says, "I will go down into *Sheol* mourning, unto my son;" though he supposed his body had been rent in pieces by wild beasts. Gen. xxxviii. 35. And at his death, the historian says, he "yielded up the ghost, and was gathered to his people;" though he was not buried with his people till seven weeks after that. Gen. xlix. 33.

"I am the God of Abraham, the God of Isaac, and the God of Jacob" (Exod. iii. 6), is interpreted by the Savior as an intimation of the future life of the spirit, since God is the God of the living, and not of the dead; and, therefore, these patriarchs were living. Matt. xxii 31, 32. And His declaration to the Sadducees, that they erred on this point, "not knowing the Scriptures," shows that those Scriptures did contain the knowledge of a future life.

So the language of David, "Thou wilt not leave my soul in hell, neither wilt thou suffer thine holy one to see corruption" (Ps. xvi 8-11), is explained by Peter as prophetic of the resurrection of Christ; which necessitates the idea of David's belief in a future existence. Acts ii

And then the several instances of a miraculous restoration to life, by Elijah and Elisha, must have suggested the thought of a separate existence of the soul. The people did not suppose that these men of God created the soul anew, and united it to the body; but only that they called it back, as it were, which of course implies its continued existence out of the body. The cases referred to are the son of the widow of Zarephath, 1 Kings xvii 17-23; the son of the Shunamite woman, 2 Kings iv. 33-36; and the man let down into the sepulcher of Elisha, 2 Kings xiii. 21.

These passages, which might be greatly multiplied, demonstrate the error of Bishop Warburton and others, who attempt to show that the earlier Hebrew Scriptures do not contain "even the idea of a future state." They certainly do, but that this idea is as clear and satisfactory as the view given in the Gospel, no one would think of affirming. There is evidently a growth in this respect, as it is easy to see that the faith of the Psalmist and the prophets is much more full and rounded than that of their ancestors. God instructed mankind by degrees, removing the darkness, and adding to their knowledge little by little, till at last Christ brought the doctrine of life and immortality out of all shadow, and set it before the world in the clear and perfect light of the Gospel.

Nothing is plainer than that God operates in the moral and spiritual world by the same method which governs His action in the physical or material world. He does not make an oak in a moment, but begins with the acorn, and causes it to grow up year by year to the perfect tree. So He does not enlighten the world all at once, by miracle, but educates them step by step, adding truth to truth, knowledge to knowledge, till the work is complete, and earth, like a mirror, reflects the light, and beauty, and blessedness of heaven.

Hence the Law is represented as the schoolmaster to bring us to Christ, who is to finish our education in the school of God, and instruct us in the perfect glory of His wisdom and truth, and in the nature and extent of His love and salvation.

The chief element of this argument will receive further elucidation in what follows.

2. "If the argument against endless misery, drawn from the silence of the Old Testament, is sound, is it not equally good against the doctrine of universal salvation?"

What has been said in the foregoing reply, regarding the method of divine instruction and revelation, has equal force in respect to this question. God does not reveal all the truth at once, but by degrees; yet at no period does He leave the world entirely in the dark, without any ray of light or hope.

In the very beginning, when the first transgression shadowed the beauty of Eden, and destroyed the innocence and happiness of our first parents, there was a voice of mercy heard, and a single star of promise rose upon the darkness of the night.

"And the Lord God said unto the serpent, I will put enmity between thee and the woman, and between thy seed and her seed; and it shall bruise thy head, and thou shalt bruise his heel." Gen. iii. 14-16. This passage is universally regarded as a promise of the Messiah, who, as the seed of the woman, should destroy the kingdom of evil, symbolized by the serpent; or, as Paul expresses it, "who took the part of flesh and blood, that through death He might destroy him that had the power of death, that is, the devil; and deliver them who, through fear of death, were all their lifetime subject to bondage." Heb. ii 14.

Of course it did not appear to Adam and Eve in the full glory with which it came, in its fulfillment, to the disciple of the Messiah Himself. Still the fact of a promise revealing the final destruction of evil, the crushing of the serpent's head, as reported by Moses, is enough to show that these unhappy transgressors were not left without some hope that their evil would be overcome of good.

Doubtless, if the original communication to them from God was couched in the language of the sacred historian, or in any similar phrase or figure, the light that fell from it was faint and dim; but any light served to keep them from utter darkness and despair. They could not learn from the promise, as it stands, when, or where, or how, the evil they had introduced into the world was to be removed, and innocence and happiness restored to them and their posterity; but, since God had spoken these words of mercy, they could not be entirely hopeless.

In Genesis V 24, we are informed that "Enoch walked with God; and he was not; for God took him." Speaking of this event, Paul says: "By faith Enoch was translated that he should not see death; and was not found, because God had translated him; for before his translation he had this testimony, that he pleased God." Heb. xi 5. Here is plainly a declaration of the continued life of the soul after removal from the earth. It is of no consequence how we interpret the manner of this translation, the record shows that the idea of a future existence was not absent from the minds of men at that period.

If it was understood that Enoch did not see death, then, of course, he lived after he left the earth; and, though nothing is said directly of the character of that life, the expression "God took him," and the peculiar character of his removal from earth, would indicate that the life to which he was called was not less desirable than that on earth. No particulars are given, it is true; nothing is specified as to the nature of this life; but the fact is left in a way to shadow forth, however dimly, something indicative of hope and expectation of a new and closer relation to God.

So the promise to Abraham: "In thee, and in thy seed, shall all the families and nations and kindreds of the earth be blessed." Gen. xii 3, xxii 18; Acts iii. 25; Gal. iii. 8. Doubtless Abraham did not comprehend the full spirit of this promise; nor should we, indeed, if the Christian apostle had not interpreted it to us; but, by faith, he saw in the distant future the dawn of a day whose brightness was to illuminate the nations, and to renew the early beauty and blessings of Eden. Like Adam and Eve, he had the promise of a great good to come, through his seed, to all the kindreds of the earth, and he rejoiced; but the nature of the blessing, the shape in which it was to come, the spiritual and heavenly direction of it, were not revealed to him. These were reserved as the special announcements of Him who gave assurance that in the resurrection we are equal unto the angels, and are children of God, being children of the resurrection. Matt. xxii; Luke xxi

And when the Preacher says, "Then shall the dust return to the earth as it was, and the spirit shall return unto God who gave it" (Ecc. xii 7), the distinction between the body and the soul is so obvious, that there is no room for doubting the writer's belief in a future life. And the statement that the spirit returns to God, though given without any specifications as to its future happiness, is surely strong presumptive proof that it would be in a heavenly state. If to be with God is indicative of good, then the spirit, returning to God, may justly be regarded as having attained to good, and that necessarily a spiritual good. Further than this the testimony does not go; but observe that the statement is general, and that whatsoever good is predicated of one soul is predicated of all.

Isaiah xxv 6-8. "And in this mountain shall the Lord of hosts make unto all people a feast of fat things...And He will destroy in this mountain the face of the covering cast over all people, and the veil spread over all nations. He will swallow up death in victory; and the Lord God will wipe away tears from off all faces; and the rebuke of His people shall He take away from off all the earth."

Paul applies this to the resurrection: "When this corruptible shall have put on incorruption, and this mortal shall have put on immortality, then shall be brought to pass the saying that is written, Death is swallowed up in victory." 1 Cor. xv 54.

We have apostolic authority, then, for saying this passage of the evangelical prophet, as Isaiah has been called, is a foreshadowing of the great doctrine of immortal life and blessedness brought into the light by the Gospel. But it is a question if Isaiah comprehended the exact nature of the blessing, or the method of its application to "all people and nations." Filled with the Holy Spirit, he seems to have forseen the distant glory of the new era under the Messiah. God permitted him, with anointed vision, to behold afar off the universal blessing which Christ was to bring to mankind; but that he saw death swallowed up in victory, with a spiritual sight as clear as Paul's, can scarcely be supposed.

Even the disciples of Jesus did not fully understand the method of the great redemption, till after the enlightenment on the day of Pentecost. And Peter must have the vision of the sheet let down from heaven, knit at the four corners, and drawn up again with all its contents, before he can be made to see that *all* peoples, Gentiles as well as Jews, come from God, and through Christ return to Him again, as His children, and not as disciples of Moses. We cannot, therefore, reasonably suppose that the Gospel plan of redemption and grace was better understood by the Hebrew prophet than by the personal disciple of Jesus.

Still it is manifest that there had been growth from Adam to Isaiah. There is a marked contrast between the figurative promise, that the serpent's head should be bruised; and the exultant language of the prophet, that all nations should share in the feast which the Lord was to prepare, under the Messiah, in the mountain of His holiness. The light of divine truth was dispensed more largely to the prophet than to the patriarch.

However dim the prophecy might have seemed to the people of that age, it appears clear enough to our minds. And yet, if we had not the inspired apostle for our interpreter, it is quite probable we should have been as much in the dark as the Jews, and have mistaken the nature of the promised blessings as widely as they have. We must judge of the clearness of these prophecies to the people of that day, not from the Christian, but from the Jewish standpoint; not by the full light of our noon-tide, but by the dim gray twilight of their morning.

Still it is certain enough that there has been light on this question, however faint, in all ages from the beginning. God has never left the world wholly under a cloud, as regards the future. As we have seen, the promise of redemption, of the final destruction of evil, and of the universal reign of good, may be traced back even up to the first transgression.

32

But, supposing it were not so, - supposing no indications of this great truth were to be found in the Old Testament, - it would not affect the argument against endless punishment. It may be perfectly consistent with justice and mercy, for a ruler to keep his own counsel in regard to any good he intends to confer on his people; but it does not follow from this that it would be equally consistent with justice and mercy, to conceal from them any great evil he intends to inflict, especially when this evil might be avoided by timely warning on his part, which warning, nevertheless, he refuses to give.

A father might purpose giving a splendid feast to all his children, but no principle of honor would be violated, he would be chargeable with no wrong toward them, if he did not inform them of the fact till the day they were invited. But if he should dig an immense pit before his door, and kindle a sulphurous fire at the bottom, and know that his children, when they came, it being night, would fall into it and perish, if he did not give them notice of it, and yet never mention the thing to them, nor give them the least hint of their danger; would this be honorable, and just, and merciful? Would they have no right to complain of this as an unheard-of wickedness?

And this is an exact statement of the difference between Universalism and endless punishment, and of the moral principles involved in the asserted silence of the Old Testament. Even if the promise to our first parents had not been given, nor that to Abraham; even if the purpose of God to destroy the reign of sin, and restore all souls to Himself, had not been mentioned at all to patriarchs or prophets; still it would only show that He intended better than He promised - that He has in store for His children greater blessings than He has ever given them reason to expect. And in this there is surely no great room for fault-finding on their part, nor for accusation against His goodness.

But, as we have shown, if He concealed from them His purpose of endless woe against those who transgressed His laws, the case is very different, and an injury is done them beyond all calculation, beside the violation of justice and honor on His part. He is like the father who digs the pit of death in the way of his children, and sees them walking straight into it, knowing that they are utterly ignorant of their danger; and knowing also that, if he had warned them, they would have turned away, and gone by some other path. For such a father, earthly or heavenly, there is no apology or defense possible.

[1] Milman's History of the Jews, vol. I 117; Warburton's Divine Legation of Moses, vol. iii. 1, 2, 10th ed. Lon.; Paley's Works, vol. V 110, Sermon xiii.; Wine's Commentaries on the Laws of the Ancient Hebrews, p. 275; Jahn's Archaeology, p. 398; Whateley's Essays on some of the Peculiarities of the Christian Religion, p. 44, 2d ed. The same argument is repeated in his Scripture Revelations concerning a Future State, pp. 18, 19, Amer. ed. For other authorities see chap. x., sect. i.
[2] I am indebted to Dr. Sawyer for these last two authorities, as cited by him in the Discussion on the Doctrine of Eternal Salvation, p. 36. For additional witnesses see chap. x., sect. ii.

[3] See chap. x., sect. i, Note 5.

[4] It is very notable how perfectly the Book of Job harmonizes with the Law in respect to rewards and punishments after death. Job's losses are made up in kind, and his virtues and integrity are rewarded with the divine approbation, peace of mind, and honor and affection from his neighbors; but not the least hint of any future reward, or of any future punishment for his wicked enemies. It is surely very mysterious, if the doctrine was revealed in the time of Job, that this remarkable moral drama should ignore it altogether; especially when, if true, it would have fallen in so admirably with the design of the author.

[5] Introduction to Job. The previous quotations are from Stuart's Essay on Future Punishment, p. 116; Lowth's Lectures on Hebrew Poetry, p. 347, and Note to page 64, Edit. 1829; Herder's Hebrew Poetry, vol. I, Dialogue viiI This work of Herder ought to be in the hands of every one who wishes to understand and to enjoy the reading of the poetical portions of the Hebrew Scriptures. It is written in a very pleasing and engaging style, and abounds in information on the subject treated.

[6] Exegetical Essays on Future Punishment, p. 113; Bush on the Resurrection, p. 93.

Chapter Three - Endless Punishment of Heathen Origin

In the previous chapters we have followed our subject through the Patriarchal and Law periods, down to the close of the Old Testament; and the inquiry has satisfactorily shown, we trust, that the doctrine of Endless Punishment is nowhere to be found in the sacred Scriptures of the Jews.

But we know that the heathen world, during a large portion of this period, was in possession of the doctrine, and fully believed it. It is pertinent to our subject, therefore, to inquire into their belief, and endeavor to ascertain from what source they obtained it. It may be, too, that the examination will discover to us the source of some of our modern doctrines on the subject. At any rate, it will show that the superstitions of the past and the present, of Pagans and Christians, are not very wide apart.

Section I. Description of the Heathen Hell

Among the ancient pagans, the belief in a hell of some sort was very general, if not universal. It was known by various names, as *Orcus, Erebus, Tartarus,* and *Infernus* or *Inferna,* whence our expression "infernal regions," &c. The views current respecting it were different at different periods, and among different nations, according to the degree of civilization, and the genius of the people. What I shall offer on this point will have respect mostly to the Romans, Greeks, and Egyptians.

1. *Its Location.* It was supposed to be as far below the earth (or as deep down in it), as the heavens are above it. Hesiod, the Greek poet, who lived 850 B.C., is very precise in his statement, and says a mass of iron would be nine days falling from heaven to earth, and nine more in falling from earth to hell. So say Apollodorus, Virgil, and others. [1]

2. *The Inhabitants.* Some idea of the natives of the country, may be gathered from the following description, taken from the Aeneid of Virgil, B. vi:

"At Hell's dread mouth a thousand *monsters* wait; -
Grief weeps, and *Vengeance* bellows in the gate;
Base *Want,* low *Fear,* and *Famine's* lawless rage.
And pale *Disease,* and slow, repining *Age:*
Fierce, formidable *Fiends* the portals keep,
With *Pain, Toil, Death,* and Death's half-brother *Sleep.*
There Joys, embittered by *Remorse,* appear,
Daughters of *Guilt;* here storms destructive *War.*
Mad *Discord* there her snaky tresses tore;
Here stretched on iron beds the *Furies* roar;
And close by *Lerna's* hissing monster stands
Briareus dreadful with a hundred hands;
There stern *Geryon* raged; and all around
Fierce *Harpies* screamed, and direful *Gorgons* frowned." [2]

Pitt's Aeneid, vi 385, &c.

The gate of Hell was guarded by the dog Cerberus, of three heads (Hesiod says fifty), who prevented all egress from the infernal regions. Once in, there was no escape. To make it still more sure, the horrid prison of hell was surrounded by a *river of fire,* called Phlegethon; within which was another security in the shape of a triple *wall.* Hence Virgil says:

"Here rolls the roaring, flaming tide of hell,
    And thundering rocks the fiery torrent swell." [3]

3. *Of the Punishments.* Virgil gives us a brief account of these in the book already quoted from:

"And now wild shouts, and wailings dire,
    And shrieking *infants* [4] swell the dreadful choir.
    Here sits in bloody robes the Fury fell,
    By night and day to watch the gates of hell.
    Here you begin terrific groans to hear,
    And sounding lashes rise upon the ear.
    On every side the damned their fetters grate,
    And curse, 'mid clanking chains, their wretched fate." [5]

A few examples of individual torments will better illustrate the subject, and reveal at the same time how inherent in them is the idea of perpetual duration.

Ixion, for a certain monstrous sin, is bound to a wheel of fire, which is ever in continual motion, in swift revolution of torment. *Tantalus,* for having attempted to deceive some of the gods who visited him, by placing roasted human flesh before them, was tortured with endless hunger and thirst. He was placed in a lake up to his chin in the water, and over his head bent the branches of a tree loaded with the most delicious and inviting fruit. Agonizing with hunger and thirst, he stretched out his hand to seize the fruit, when it was instantly withdrawn just above his reach; he stooped to drink of the cooling waters, and immediately they sank away, and no drop touched his lips; but they rose again to his chin, when he rose. [From this comes our word "tantalize."]

The fifty *Daughters of Danaus,* or rather forty-nine, for murdering their husbands on the night of marriage, were condemned to fill a leaky tub with water drawn from a deep well with a sieve. Of course there was no end to such a task. *Sisyphus* was condemned to roll a huge stone to the summit of a high hill in hell, but always, just before he reached the top, his strength failed, and it rushed down again to the bottom of the steep, and compelled him to begin his labors again, always to end in the same way. Another miserable wretch had a mighty rock suspended over his head, threatening every instant to fall and crush him. *Tityrus,* for his crimes, was chained to a rock, while a vulture fed upon his heart and entrails, which were ever renewed as fast as devoured. [6]

These examples are sufficient to illustrate the doctrines and teachings of the heathen respecting future punishments; and they show, more graphically than any words could do it, how essential to their completeness is the element of perpetuity, of endlessness. There can be no doubt in respect to *their* belief in the torments of the wicked after death, or of their opinion respecting the duration of them.

The fact, then, being established, that the dogma is thoroughly heathen in its character and developments, this question presents itself: Where did the heathen get it? Whence came their fables respecting the infernal regions? The next section will answer this inquiry.

Section II. The Heathen Invented the Doctrine of Endless Punishment - Shown by Their Own Confessions

Any one at all familiar with the writings of the ancient Greeks or Romans, cannot fail to note how often it is admitted by them that the national religions were the inventions of the legislator and the priest, for the purpose of governing and restraining the common people. Hence, all the early lawgivers claim to have had communications with the gods, who aided them in the preparation of their codes. Zoroaster claimed to have received his laws from a divine source; Lycurgus obtained his from Apollo, Minos of Crete from Jupiter, Numa of Rome from Egeria, Zaleucus from Minerva, &c. The object of this sacred fraud was to impress the minds of the multitude with religious awe, and command a more ready obedience on their part. Hence Augustine says, in his "City of God," "This seems to have been done on no other account, but as it was the business of princes, out of their wisdom and civil prudence, to deceive the people in their religion; princes, under the name of religion, persuaded the people to believe those things true, which they themselves knew to be idle fables; by this means, for their own ease in government, tying them the more closely to civil society." B. iv. 32.

Of course, in order to secure obedience, they were obliged to invent divine punishments for the disobedience of what they asserted to be divine laws. "Hence," says Bishop Warburton, "they enforced the belief of a future state of rewards and punishments by every sort of contrivance." And speaking of the addition of metempsychosis, or the transmigration of souls, he says: "This was an ingenious solution, invented by the Egyptian lawgivers, to remove all doubts concerning the moral attributes of God."

Egypt has been called the "Mother of Superstitions," and her whole religious history shows the propriety of the appellation. Greeks and Romans, Lawgivers and Philosophers, acknowledge their indebtedness to her in this respect, and freely credit her with the original invention of the fables and terrors of the invisible world; though it must be allowed that they have improved somewhat upon the hints given, and shown a wonderful inventive faculty of their own.

Dr. Good has a curious passage on the subject in hand, in his Book of Nature, which I must be permitted to introduce here. "It was believed in most countries," he says, "that this hell, *hades,* or invisible world, is divided into two very distinct and opposite regions, by a broad and impassable gulf; that the one is a seat of happiness, a paradise, or elysium, and the other a seat of misery, a gehenna, or tartarus; and that there is a supreme magistrate and an impartial tribunal belonging to the infernal shades, before which the ghosts must appear, and by which they are sentenced to the one or the other, according to the deeds done in the body. Egypt is said to have been the inventress of this important and valuable part of the tradition; and undoubtedly it is to be found in the earliest records of Egyptian history. But, from the wonderful conformity of its outlines to the parallel doctrines of the Scriptures, it is probable that it has a still higher origin, and that it constituted a part of the patriarchal creed, retained in a few channels, though forgotten or obliterated in others, and consequently that it was a divine communication in a very early age." [7]

This last assertion is certainly a singular statement for a man of Dr. Good's learning and judgment. For, *first,* it does not conform at all to the doctrine of the Scriptures in regard to rewards and punishments, as our inquiry has fully shown. And, *second,* the patriarchal creed makes no mention of it, as far as we know; and if it made part of an early revelation, afterwards lost, it is reasonable to suppose that it would have been renewed again in the revelation to the Law of Moses.

Beside, if the Egyptians obtained it from any of the patriarchs, it must have been from Jacob or his descendants, after they went down into Egypt. It must have been a current doctrine, therefore, among the Israelites, and regarded by them as of divine authority; but this conclusion is shut off by the fact that Moses, though divinely commissioned as their teacher, rejects it from his law, and shows his unbelief and contempt for it by a studied and unbroken silence! Curious, indeed, if Dr. Good's supposition is correct. We find the doctrine in full bloom with the Egyptians, but not a trace of it among the early Hebrews. But, singularly enough, when, in after ages, the Jews had become corrupted, and had departed from the Law of Moses, we find the doctrine among them. And, what is very noteworthy, as the next chapter will show, its first appearance is in apocryphal books written by *Egyptian* Jews. So that the facts happen to be the very opposite of Dr. Good's theory; - instead of the Egyptians borrowing it from the Jews, the Jews borrowed it from the Egyptians.

In attempting to set out the Egyptian notions on the subject, it is difficult to choose between the conflicting accounts of the Greek writers, Herodotus, Diodorus Siculus, Plutarch, &c., as well as of the modern interpreters of the monumental hieroglyphics. Still, with regard to the main question, they are tolerably well agreed, though there is great diversity of opinion in respect to the details. It is plain enough, from their united testimony, that the whole matter of judgment after death, the rewards of a good life, and the punishments of a bad life, with all the formal solemnities of trial and condemnation, originated and was perfected among the Egyptians, according to the peculiar character of their mythology. From them it was borrowed by the Greeks, who made such changes and additions as fitted the system to the genius and circumstances of that people.

It would seem that each district of Egypt had what was called its "sacred lake," beyond which were the tombs and burial-places of the dead. Acherusia, the lake near Memphis, was the model probably for the rest, and appears to have furnished a general name for them.

When any one died, it was the duty of his relations, according to Diodorus, to notify the forty-two judges or assessors, whose office it was to decide upon the character of the deceased, and then to appoint the day for the funeral ceremonies and burial. When the day came, the body of the dead was carried in procession to the shore of the lake, from which it could not be removed till after the judgment. The forty-two judges, having been summoned, were in waiting at the place of embarkation, to receive the body, and enter on the trial. It was then lawful, for any person who thought proper, to bring charges against the deceased; and if it was proved that he had led an evil life, the judges condemned him for his wickedness, and refused him the privilege of burial, which was regarded as one of the greatest possible calamities. But if those accusing the dead failed to establish their accusations, they were subjected to the heaviest penalties.

If there was no accuser, or the charges were disproved, then his relations were allowed to pronounce the accustomed eulogy, praising his piety and goodness, celebrating his virtues, and declaring the excellent life which he had lived. This was followed by a prayer supplicating the gods of the underworld to receive him into the society of the blessed. Then came the acclamations of the multitude assembled on the occasion, who united in extolling the character of the dead, and in rejoicing that he was now going to join the virtuous in the regions of *Amenti* or *Hades.*

This over, the body was placed in the funeral boat, under the direction of *Horus,* the ferryman of the dead, and borne across the lake to its place of sepulture. This done, the ceremonies of the occasion closed.

The bodies of those who had been refused burial were carried back by the family, and the coffins set up against the wall of the house. The spirit could not be at rest until the body was buried. "The duration of this punishment was limited," says Wilkinson, "according to the extent of crimes of which the accused had been guilty. When the devotion of friends, aided by liberal donations in the service of religion, and the influential prayers of the priests, had sufficiently softened the otherwise inexorable nature of the gods, the period of this state of purgatory was doubtless shortened." [8]

Beside this judgment on earth, it appears there was another after the dead entered the regions of *Amenti* or *Hades.* For what reason, we cannot say, except the judges of the invisible world were a kind of superior court, who examined the case anew, with the view of correcting any errors of the previous trial.

Sir J.G. Wilkinson informs us that "the judgment scenes found in the tombs and on the papyri, sometimes represent the deceased conducted by Horus to the region of Amenti, Cerberus is present as the guardian of the gates, near which the scales of justice were erected. Anubis, 'the director of the weight,' having placed a vase representing the good actions, or the heart of the deceased, in one scale, and the figure or emblem of truth in the other, proceeds to ascertain his claims for admission. If, on being 'weighed,' he is 'found wanting,' he is rejected; and Osiris, the judge of the dead, inclining the scepter in token of condemnation, pronounces judgment upon him, and condemns his soul to return to earth under the form of a pig, or some other unclean animal. Placed in a boat, it is removed, under the charge of two monkeys, from the precincts of Amenti, all communication with which is figuratively cut off by a man who hews away the earth with an ax after its passage; and the commencement of a new term of life is indicated by the monkeys, the emblems of Thoth, as Time. But if, when the sum of his deeds have been recorded, his virtues so far predominate as to entitle him to admission to the mansions of the blessed, Horus introduces him to Osiris." [9]

It is with this judgment, at the point where the condemned soul is sent back again to the earth in the form of an animal, that the doctrine of transmigration seems to connect itself.

According to Herodotus, the Egyptians believed the soul would pass from one body to another, till it had performed the circuit of all animals, terrestrial, marine, and birds of the air; when it again takes up its abode in the human body. This transmigration it was supposed would fill up a period of three thousand years.

There is great diversity of opinion in regard to the particulars of this curious arrangement, but the leading idea appears to have been the punishment of the wicked; for the wicked only, according to some authorities, were subject to it, the good and pious being received immediately, on the burial of the body, into rest, or returning to the Good Being whence they emanated. And it would seem, according to Wilkinson, that it was only the ordinarily wicked, not the very worst, who were condemned to this purgatory. He thinks that the monuments show "that the souls which underwent transmigration were those of men whose sins were of a sufficiently moderate kind to admit of that purification; the unpardonable sinner being condemned to eternal fire," by which he means endless fire.

These records of the ancient Greeks, confirmed by the monuments as illustrated by modern scholars, open to us the origin of the doctrines of a judgment after death, and of future endless rewards and punishments, for the good or evil deeds of this life. From the Egyptians it passed, with suitable modifications, to the Greeks and Romans. Diodorus himself clearly shows that the fables of the Acherusian lake, of Hecate, Cerberus, Charon, and the Styx, have their original in these Egyptian ceremonies and doctrines.

And Professor Stuart, in a note to Greppo's Essay on Hieroglyphics, accepts the statement of Spineto, that the *Amenti* of the Egyptians originated the classic fables of Hades and Tartarus, Charon, Pluto, the judges of hell, the dog Cerberus, the Chimeras, Harpies, Gorgons, Furies, "and other such unnatural and horrible things with which the Greeks and Romans peopled their fantastic hell."

It is curious to note the exactness of the copy in many particulars. The Egyptian *Acherusia* gives us the Greek *Acheron,* and perhaps *Styx.* The Egyptian *Tartar,* significant of the lamentations of relatives over the dead refused burial on account of their wicked lives, furnishes the Greek *Tartarus,* where the wicked are punished. The funeral boat across the lake, the ferryman, and the gold piece in the mouth of the dead, give rise to Charon, his boat, and fee, and the passage across the Styx into Hades. The cemetery beyond the lake, surrounded by trees, called by the Egyptians *Elisout* or *Elisaeus,* is the original of the Greek *Elysian Fields,* the abode of the blessed. The three infernal judges, *Minos, Aeacus, Rhadamanthus,* are borrowed from the Egyptian judges of the dead; and the heads of animals symbolizing these judges, mistaken by the Greeks, are changed into monster *Gorgons, Harpies, Furies,* &c.

40

But, as I have remarked, though the Greeks borrowed, they altered and improved. And, true to that individualism which was so marked a characteristic of that people, they are not satisfied with the Egyptian method of generalizing respecting the punishments of the wicked, but begin specifying particular sinners, and particular kinds of punishment adapted to particular offenses. Hence the fables of Ixion, Tantalus, Tityrus, &c., whose torments in the infernal regions are mentioned in the beginning of this chapter. Everything must be sharp, pointed, and dramatic, to suit the lively genius of the Greek; and the terrors of the invisible world must be presented in a way to strike the imagination in the most powerful manner, and produce some direct result on the individual and on society.

The whole thing is designed for effect, to influence the multitude, to restrain their passions, and to aid the magistrate and ruler in keeping them subject to authority. It is the invention of priests and law-makers, who take this as the easiest method of governing the people. They claim the "right divine" to govern; claim that their laws originate with the gods, as we have shown above; and that, therefore, the gods will visit on all offenders the terrors and tortures of the damned. Hence, through the joint cunning of priest and legislator, of church and state, mutually supporting each the other, we have all the stupendous frauds and falsehoods respecting the invisible world.

But, without further remarks of my own, I will introduce the testimony of the heathen themselves on this point, and those the best informed among them, who will tell their own story in their own way. One preliminary observation, however, partly made already, I wish to repeat; and I desire the reader to have it always in mind: The rulers and magistrates, or priests, invent these terrors to keep the people, the masses, in subjection; the people religiously believe in them; while the inventors, of course, and the educated classes, the priests and the philosophers, though they teach them to the multitude, have themselves no manner of faith in them.

1. *Polybius,* the historian, says: "Since the multitude is ever fickle, full of lawless desires, irrational passions and violence, there is no other way to keep them in order but by the fear and terror of the invisible world; on which account our ancestors seem to me to have acted judiciously, when they contrived to bring into the popular belief these notions of the gods, and of the infernal regions." B. vi 56.

2. *Dionysius Halicarnassus* treats the whole matter as useful, but not as true. *Antiq. Rom.,* B. ii

3. *Livy,* the celebrated historian, speaks of it in the same spirit; and he praises the wisdom of Numa, because he invented the fear of the gods, as "a most efficacious means of governing an ignorant and barbarous populace." *Hist.,* I 19.

4. *Strabo,* the geographer, says: "The multitude are restrained from vice by the punishments the gods are said to inflict upon offenders, and by those terrors and threatenings which certain dreadful words and monstrous forms imprint upon their minds...For it is impossible to govern the crowd of wom-

en, and all the common rabble, by philosophical reasoning, and lead them to piety, holiness and virtue - but this must be done by superstition, or the fear of the gods, by means of fables and wonders; for the thunder, the aegis, the trident, the torches (of the Furies), the dragons, &c., are all fables, as is also all the ancient theology. These things the legislators used as scarecrows to terrify the childish multitude." *Geog.,* B. I

5. *Timaeus Locrus,* the Pythagorean, after stating that the doctrine of rewards and punishments after death is necessary to society, proceeds as follows: "For as we sometimes cure the body with unwholesome remedies, when such as are most wholesome produce no effect, so we restrain those minds with false relations, which will not be persuaded by the truth. There is a necessity, therefore, of instilling the dread of those *foreign* torments: [10] as that the soul changes its habitation; that the coward is ignominiously thrust into the body of a woman; the murderer imprisoned within the form of a savage beast; the vain and inconstant changed into birds, and the slothful and ignorant into fishes."

6. *Plato,* in his commentary on Timaeus, fully endorses what he says respecting the fabulous invention of these foreign torments. And Strabo says that "Plato and the Brahmins of India invented fables concerning the future judgments of hell" (Hades). And Chrysippus blames Plato for attempting to deter men from wrong by frightful stories of future punishments.

Plato himself is exceedingly inconsistent, sometimes adopting, even in his serious discourses, the fables of the poets, and at other times rejecting them as utterly false, and giving too frightful views of the invisible world. Sometimes, he argues, on social grounds, that they are necessary to restrain bad men from wickedness and crime, and then again he protests against them on political grounds, as intimidating the citizens, and making cowards of the soldiers, who, believing these things, are afraid of death, and do not therefore fight well. But all this shows in what light he regarded them; not as truths, certainly, but as fictions, convenient in some cases, but difficult to manage in others.

7. *Plutarch* treats the subject in the same way; sometimes arguing for them with great solemnity and earnestness, and on other occasions calling them "fabulous stories, the tales of mothers and nurses."

8. *Seneca* says: "Those things which make the infernal regions terrible, the darkness, the prison, the river of flaming fire, the judgment seat, &c., are all a fable, with which the poets amuse themselves, and by them agitate us with vain terrors." *Sextus Empiricus* calls them "poetic fables of hell;" and *Cicero* speaks of them as "silly absurdities and fables" (*ineptiis ac fabulis*).

9. *Aristotle.* "It has been handed down in mythical form from earliest times to posterity, that there are gods, and that the divine (Deity) compasses all nature. All beside this has been added, after the mythical style, for the purpose of persuading the multitude, and for the interests of the laws, and the advantage of the state." *Neander's Church Hist.,* I, p. 7. [11]

The question with which this section began, "Whence came the doctrine of future endless punishments?" is now, I trust, answered by a sufficient number of witnesses to settle the matter beyond dispute. The heathens themselves confess to the invention of the dogma, and of all the fabulous stories of the infernal regions; the legislators and sages very frankly state that the whole thing was devised for its supposed utility in governing the gross and ignorant multitude of men and women, who cannot be restrained by the precepts of philosophy. [12]

They have not the slightest faith in these things themselves; they do not think them at all necessary to regulate their own lives, or keep them in order; but it is for the common people, the coarse rabble, who can only in this way be terrified into good behavior. One cannot help noting the resemblance between these wise men and some of our own day, who seem so anxious to maintain the doctrine in the ground that it is necessary to restrain men from sin. But, unfortunately for this theory, the revelations of history, both Pagan and Christian, are all in opposition to it.

[1] A Catholic Catechism, reviewed by the London Athenaeum, has the following questions and answers: "Q. Where is hell? A. It is in the middle of the earth. Q. Is hell very large? A. Not very; for the damned lay packed in it one upon another, like the bricks in a brick oven." Our Protestant brethren are not quite so precise in locating the place. "Hell is in any place where God chooses to have it; or where sinners choose to have it; or where devils make it. Or it may be in some planet, or between the planets; or it may be in no particular place. It may be everywhere but in heaven. *Hell is infinite misery.* Wherever infinite misery is endured is hell. If, to produce this, it is necessary to put all wicked men into one pit, they will be put there; if not, they may have more room." - *New York Observer.*

[2] This harmonizes very well with the Christian view on this head; for, beside the devil and countless legions of demons as inhabitants, we have, according to an Orthodox poet,

"Pale phantoms, hideous specters, shapes which scare
The damned themselves, and terrify despair.
'Gorgons and Harpies, and Chimeras dire,'
And swarms of twisted serpents, hissing fire."

And Erasmus speaks of "spiritual lions and bears," "scorpions, snakes and dragons, to wit, spirits who creep round and look continually on the damned firebrands of hell."

[3] This also is copied by the Christian delineator:

"Fires spout in cataracts, or in *rivers* flow -
In bubbling eddies rolls the *fiery tide,*
And sulfurous surges on each other ride."

Dr. Trapp.

"Suddenly before my eye
A *wall* of fiery adamant sprung up -
Wall mountainous, tremendous, flaming high
Above all flight of hope."

Pollock.

[4] Here, too, both Catholic and Protestant strike hands with the heathen, and borrow from them the detestable dogma of infant damnation, which, as seen above, is older than Calvinism or Catholicism. "The condemnation of children dying without having been baptized," says the Catholic Bossuet, "is an article of firm faith of the church. They are guilty, since they die in the wrath of God, and in the powers of darkness. Children of wrath by nature, objects of hatred and aversion, cast into hell with the other damned, they remain there everlastingly subject to the horrible vengeance of the devil. Thus the learned Denis Peteau has decided, as well as the most eminent Bellarmin, the Council of Lyons, the Council of Florence, and the Council of Trent."

"How comes it to pass that the fall of Adam, *without remedy,* should involve so many nations, with their *infant children,* in eternal death, but because of the will of God? It is a horrible decree, I confess!" - *Calvin's Institutes,* Book iii., c. 23, 7.

[5] So the Christian poets describe their hell, employing the same language, as Drs. Trapp and Young below:

"The *clank of chains,*
  The clang of *lashing whips,* shrill *shrieks* and *groans,*
  Loud, ceaseless howlings, cries and piercing moans."
"Where shrieks, the roaring flame, the rattling chain,
  And all the dreadful eloquence of pain."

The correspondences which I have italicized, and the theft, are equally obvious.

[6] The above methods of torment display a commendable degree of inventive genius; but the following, taken from a Christian(?) Orthodox sermon, exceeds in devilish ingenuity and torture anything to be found in the heathen hell. So far, therefore, it is an improvement on the original:

"How black are the Fiends! How furious are their Tormentors! 'Tis their only music to hear their miserable patients roar, to hear their bones crack. 'Tis their meat and drink to see how their flesh rieth, and their fat droppeth; to drench them with burning metal, and to rip open their bodies, and to pour in fierce burning brass into their bowels and the recesses and ventricles of their hearts. What thinkest thou of those chains of darkness, those instruments of cruelty? Canst thou be content to burn? Seest thou how the worm gnaweth, how the oven gloweth, how the fire rageth? What sayest thou to that river of brimstone, that gulf of perdition? Wilt thou take up thy habitation there? O, lay thine ear to the door of hell! Hearest thou the curses and blasphemies, the weepings and wailings, how they lament their follies, and curse their day; how they do roar and yell, and gnash their teeth; how deep are their groans; how feeling are their moans; how inconceivable are their miseries? If the shrieks of *Korah, Dathan,* and *Abiram,* were so terrible (when the earth clave asunder and opened its

44

mouth and swallowed them up, and all that appertained to them) that all *Israel* fled at the cry to them; O, how fearful would the cry be, if God should take off the covering of the mouth of hell, and let the cry of the damned ascend in all its terror among the children of men, and of all their moans and miseries this the piercing killing emphasis and burden, *forever! forever!"*

[7] Harpers' Edit., p. 338. See, also, the Egyptian origin of the doctrine abundantly proved in Warburton's Divine Legation, to which I am indebted for several of the authorities given in this section, with quotations from the original text. Also Leland on the Necessity of Divine Revelation, Part III, chaps. i-viii. The supposed beginning and growth of the doctrine among the Egyptians is briefly shown by Heeren, Historical Researches, African Nations, vol. ii 189-199, 2d Edit. It is well worthy of a careful perusal. See also Book of the Dead in Bibliotheca Sacra for 1868, pp. 69-112.

[8] Here unquestionably is the germ of the Catholic purgatory. The "liberal donations" and "the prayers of the priests" are family features too marked to be mistaken.

[9] Wilkinson's Ancient Egyptians, Chap. x. Harpers' Edit. vol. ii pp. 356-400. See also Bohn's Pictorial Dictionary of the Bible, and Ree's Cyclopedia, Art. *Egypt.* American Encyclopedia, Art. *Hieroglyphics.*

[10] The Greeks and Romans, when speaking of religious things, usually employ the word "foreign" to mean Egyptian. The doctrine was imported into Greece by the lawgivers and philosophers, who traveled into Egypt in order to learn its wisdom, and to be initiated into its world-renowned mysteries.

[11] The poet Ovid in the 15th Book of his Metamorphoses, alluding to the doctrine of transmigration, states the case as follows: -

"O you, whom horrors of cold death affright,
  Why fear you Styx, vain names, and endless night,
  The dreams of poets, and feigned miseries
  Of forged hell? Whether last flames surprise,
  Or age your bodies waste, they do not grieve,
  Nor suffer pains. Our souls forever live,
  Yet evermore their ancient houses leave
  To live in new, which them as guests receive:
  All alter, nothing finally decays.
  Hither and thither still the spirit strays;
  Guests to all bodies, out of beasts it flies
  To man, from men to beasts, and never dies.
  As pliant wax each new impression takes,
  Fixed to no form, but still the old forsakes,
  Yet is the same: so souls the same abide,
  Though various bodies may the sameness hide."

[12] Montesquieu has a valuable tract on the subject of this chapter, entitled "*La Politique Des Romains dans la Religion.*" He says distinctly that the Romans "made religion for the state," and that "Romulus, Tatius and Numa, enslaved the gods to politics" (*asservirent les dieux a la Politique*).

Chapter Four - The Jews Borrowed the Doctrine from the Heathen

It is allowed on all hands that the Jews in our Savior's time believed the doctrine of future endless punishment; that it was a part of the common faith. Of course, as the doctrine is nowhere to be found in their Scriptures, the question arises, where did they find it? At the close of the Old Testament Scriptures they did not believe it; at the beginning of the New they did.

Between these two points of time there was an interval of some four hundred years, during which there was no prophet in Israel. Malachi was the last of the Hebrew prophets, and from him to Christ there stretches this waste period of four centuries, when the Jews were without any divine teacher or revelation from heaven. And all this while they were in constant and close intercourse with the heathen, especially the Egyptians, the Greeks and Romans, who held the doctrine in review as part of the national faith. From these, therefore, they must have borrowed it, for it is certain that they could not have obtained it from any inspired source, since none was open to them during this period.

Beside, they were, all this time, as one might infer from their previous history, departing further and further from the law, and growing more and more corrupt; till at last they had, as the Savior charges upon them, utterly made void the law of God by their traditions. Mark viii. 9, 13.

Brucker says that "after the times of Esdras, Zachariah, Malachi, and the inspired men, the Jews began to forsake the sacred doctrine, and turned aside to the dreams of human invention (*humani ingenii somnia*); though up to this time they had preserved pure the Hebrew wisdom received from the fathers." [1]

The last part of this statement is, perhaps, too strongly worded. They did not, certainly, preserve the wisdom of their ancestors, and the sacred doctrine *pure,* till after the times of Malachi and the close of the prophetic period. Their departure from the simplicity of the law dates further back than this, even to the time of the Babylonian captivity. The oriental philosophy made considerable impression on the general as well as on the speculative mind, and by degrees crumbled down the walls that guarded the sanctuary of the ancient faith, and prepared the way for the general corruption which followed the death of the last of the prophets. A careful study of the later books of the Old Testament will show this very plainly.

Speaking on this point, Guizot has the following: "The Jews had acquired at Babylon a great number of Oriental notions, and their theological opinions had undergone great changes by this intercourse. We find in Ecclesiasticus, and the Wisdom of Solomon, and the later prophets, notions unknown to the Jews before the Babylonian captivity, which are manifestly derived from the Orientals. Thus, God represented under the image of light, and the principle of evil under that of darkness; the history of good and bad angels; *paradise* and *hell*, &c., are doctrines of which the origin, or at least the positive determination, can only be referred to the Oriental philosophy." [2]

Thus we see that the cords which bound them to the authority of Moses, and to the written law and revelations of God, had been slowly relaxing for a long time. Of course, when the last prophet had departed, and God had withdrawn all special guidance, the growth of corruption among them, and conformity to Pagan opinions, rapidly increased.

The process is easily understood. About three hundred and thirty years before Christ, Alexander the Great had subjected to his rule the whole of Western Asia, including Judea, and also the kingdom of Egypt. Soon after he founded Alexandria, which speedily became a great commercial metropolis, and drew into itself a large multitude of Jews, who were always eager to improve the opportunities of traffic and trade. A few years later, Ptolemy Soter took Jerusalem, and carried off one hundred thousand of them into Egypt. Here, of course, they were in daily contact with Egyptians and Greeks, and gradually began to adopt their philosophical and religious opinions, or to modify their own in harmony with them.

"To what side soever they turned," says a careful writer, "the Jews came in contact with Greeks and with Greek philosophy, under one modification or another. It was around them and among them; for small bodies of that people were scattered through their own territories, as well as through the surrounding provinces. It insinuated itself very slowly at first; but stealing upon them from every quarter, and operating from age to age, it mingled at length in all their views, and by the year 150 before Christ, had wrought a visible change in their notions and habits of thought." [3]

At Alexandria, too, was established that celebrated school of philosophy and theology which exerted such a corrupting influence on both Jewish and Christian doctrine and teaching.

"This school," says Enfield, "by pretending to teach a sublimer doctrine concerning God and divine things, enticed men of different countries and religions, and among the rest the Jews, to study its mysteries, and incorporate them with their own...Hence, under the cloak of symbols, Pagan philosophy gradually crept into the Jewish schools; and the Platonic doctrines, mixed first with the Pythagoric, and afterwards with the Egyptian and Oriental, were blended with the ancient faith in their explanations of the law and their traditions."

"This corruption, which began in the time of Ptolemy Philadelphus (B.C. 283), soon spread into Palestine, and everywhere disseminated among the Jews a taste for metaphysical subtleties and mysteries." Again, he says: "Under the Ptolemies the Jews began to learn the Egyptian and Oriental *theology*, and to incorporate those foreign dogmas with their ancient creed." And once more he says: "Some among them were so unfaithful to their country and their God, as to court the favor of the conqueror (Antiochus Epiphanes), by mixing Pagan tenets and superstitions with their own sacred doctrines and ceremonies." [4]

In these extracts we have some very important facts in aid of our inquiry. "The Pagan philosophy gradually crept into the Jewish schools," and the Jews incorporated into their ancient faith the dogmas of both the philosophy and theology of Egypt, the very fountain-head from which came the doctrine of future endless torments. But not only did they borrow from the Egyptian, but also from the Oriental and Pythagorean philosophy, in both of which, as well as in the Egyptian, one of the distinguishing features was the doctrine of metempsychosis, or the transmigration of souls, as a method of retribution after death. Indeed, Pythagoras made so much of this dogma, that it was often called specially by his name; and it was almost universally believed by the Oriental nations, and is to this day, especially by the Hindus, the Burmans, the followers of the Grand Lama, and by the Buddhists generally.

As this particular doctrine has an important bearing on our inquiry, it may be well to enlarge a little on this point. The opinions of the Egyptians have already been stated. Pythagoras taught that souls were sent into bodies corresponding to their several characters. The good were allowed to inhabit those of a gentle and social kind, as bees, doves, ants, &c. The bad were sent into such as resembled them in disposition and life; the angry and malicious into serpents; the ravenous and robbing into wolves; the fraudulent into foxes; and, with the incivility of a Mahometan, cowards and effeminate into the bodies of women.

The Buddhists, according to Judson, believe that mankind pass into other bodies, the character of which is determined by their conduct in the present life. They may be sent into the bodies of birds, beasts, fish, or insects, from a higher to a lower grade, if wicked, until they reach hell, or a place of unmixed torment. In cases of atrocious crime, as the murder of a parent, or a priest, they pass through no transmigration, but go directly to hell. [5]

This, it will be seen, corresponds with what Wilkinson says of the Egyptian doctrine, that only those sinners whose crimes admit of purification are allowed the benefit of this purgatorial transmigration, while the unpardonable sinner is condemned to endless fire.

The Hindus have brought the doctrine to such a degree of perfection, that they profess to be able "to tell precisely the sin which the person committed in another body, by the afflictions which he endures in this. For instance, they say the headache is a punishment for having, in a former state, spoken irreverently to father or mother. Madness or insanity is a punishment for having been disobedient to parents, or to the priest or spiritual guide. Epilepsy is the penalty for having in another body administered poison to any one at the command of a master. Pain in the eyes is retribution for having, when in a former body, coveted another man's wife. Blindness is a punishment for having killed one's mother; but this person, before coming into another body, will be subjected to many years' torment in hell." [6]

Such are the views respectively of the Egyptians, Pythagoreans, and Orientals, on the subject of transmigration as a system of retribution beyond death. And from these sources Enfield and others say the Jews borrowed largely, incorporating the dogmas both of their philosophy and theology with the sacred doctrines of their ancient creed. Is there any proof that they borrowed the particular doctrine in question? We answer, there is abundant proof, which we will proceed to offer.

Of course, in doing this, we shall not distinguish between the particularly Egyptian and the particularly Grecian elements. Indeed, they were so blended after the conquest of Egypt by Alexander, and the influx of Greeks into the country, that it would be next to impossible to separate the two in their influence on the Jewish mind and opinions. In presenting the evidence, we shall do with the Jews as we did by the heathen - let them speak for themselves.

In the apocryphal Book of Wisdom, written perhaps from fifty to ninety years before Christ, by an Egyptian Jew, we have the following: "I was a witty child, and had a good spirit. Yea, rather, being good, I came into a body undefiled." Chapter viii. 19, 20.

Josephus, who wrote about one hundred and fifty years later, says of the Pharisees: "They believe that souls have an immortal vigor in them, and that under the earth (in *Sheol* or *Hades*) there will be rewards and punishments, according as they have lived virtuously or viciously in this life. The latter are to be detained in an everlasting prison; but the former shall have power to revive and live again." This, it will be seen, is a great advance on the Old Testament *Sheol* or under-world. We find nothing of this sort among the patriarchs or prophets.

Again he says: "The souls of the pure and obedient obtain a most holy place in heaven, from whence, in the revolution of ages, they are again sent into pure bodies;" while the souls of those committing suicide "are received into the darkest place in Hades."

Once more: "All souls are incorruptible, but the souls of good men only are removed into other bodies; but the souls of bad men are subject to eternal punishment." [7]

These testimonies are sufficient to show how thoroughly the doctrine of transmigration had fixed itself in the Jewish creed by the time of Christ.

It will be seen that the extracts indicate that transmigration, or permission to enter other bodies on earth, was regarded by the Pharisees and Jews as a reward of virtue and goodness; while the privilege was denied to the wicked, who were kept in the under-world, or Hades, subject to punishment. It is probable that the silent, inactive, and gloomy character of Sheol, or the under-world, of the early Hebrews, which we have already described at large (chap. ii, sec. V), may have given this form to the doctrine among the Jews, and caused them to regard deliverance from it into the cheerful life of earth a favor and a reward.

It certainly was a common opinion with many, and that as far back as the second Book of Maccabees, perhaps 150 B.C., that the wicked would be punished, by being deprived of a resurrection, or confined in the under-world as shadowy ghosts, without action or enjoyment (chapters vii, xiV). This is, I think, the first glimpse we have of future punishment among the Jews, coming, as we see, not in the form of torment, but of a refusal of the privilege of a resurrection.

This doctrine has prevailed extensively among the Jews. David Kimchi (A.D. 1240) says: "The benefit of the rain is common to the just and to the unjust, but the resurrection of the dead is the peculiar privilege of those who have lived righteously." Moses Gerundensis says: "No one can be partaker of an interest in the world to come, but the souls only of just men, which, separated from their body, shall enter into it." Manasseh Ben Israel, in a treatise on the resurrection of the dead, says: "From the mind and opinion of all the ancients, we conclude that there will not be a general resurrection of the dead, and one common to all men." Pocoke has brought a large mass of evidence from Rabbinical writers to prove this point. [8]

The assertion of Ben Israel, that this was "the mind and opinion of all the ancients," is probably too broad for the facts; but it shows that at a very early period this notion had taken place in the Jewish belief. The second Book of Maccabees, written two hundred and fifty years after Malachi, shows that it was held at that period.

Still this was not the universal opinion, for evidently transmigration in the time of Christ was regarded by some as a method of punishment. Hence, in the account of the blind man restored to sight by Jesus, we have the question: "Master, who did sin, this man, or his parents, that he was born blind?" John ix. This shows plainly that the people thought the man might have been sent into a blind body as a punishment for some sin in a preexistent state; which is an exact copy of the Egyptian and Oriental doctrine.

In Luke xvi 14, we have another trace of the doctrine among the people. In answer to the question of Jesus, "Whom do men say that I, the son of man, am?" the disciples reply, "Some say that thou art John the Baptist; some say Elias; and others Jeremias, or one of the prophets." They seemed to think the soul of some one of these ancient men of God had returned again to the earth in the body of Jesus, which to them was a satisfactory explanation of the miracles He wrought. Many of the Jewish doctors have believed that the souls of Adam, Abraham, and others, have at different times animated the bodies of the great men of their nation.

It is not easy to see how those alluded to by the disciples could believe the soul of John Baptist, who had so recently been put to death, could have entered into the body of Jesus, who was thirty years old. But then the ideas of the common people on this subject, as well as of the learned, were very much mixed and confused; and, moreover, there was every variety of opinion respecting the moral theory of the system.

The Egyptians believed in transmigration as a punishment of vice; the Pharisees believed in it as a reward of virtue; and the Pythagoreans believed in it both as a reward and a punishment. The Egyptians excluded the extremely wicked; and the Pharisees excluded the wicked generally, who were punished in the under-world; while Pythagoras excluded the extremely good, or pure and philosophical souls, who were sent directly to heaven, or the society of the gods. So great was the diversity of opinion in regard even to the leading features of the system.

Philo, an Egyptian Jew contemporary with the Savior, believed the air to be full of spirits, who from time to time descended "to unite themselves with mortal bodies, being desirous to live in them again." And Josephus reports the Essenes, one of the three chief sects among the Jews, as holding the same views in regard to the preexistence of spirits, which is in fact equivalent to transmigration. [9]

A sufficient number of witnesses has now been cited to prove that the Jews borrowed from the Pagans the doctrine of transmigration, with all its accompaniments of future retribution, and endless punishment. And they abundantly justify the statement of Enfield, that "the purity of the divine doctrine was corrupted among the Jews in Egypt, who, under the disguise of allegory, admitted doctrines never dreamed of by their lawgiver and prophets; and adopted a mystical interpretation of the law, which converted its plain meaning into a thousand idle fancies."

But other views of punishments after death were entertained, approaching nearer to the crude notions exhibited in the preceding chapter. The apocryphal book, called the Wisdom of Solomon, written from fifty to seventy years later than the second of Maccabees, contains the doctrine of future retribution in a more positive form. The habitation of the wicked is in darkness and amid terrors, and the Almighty turns all the elements against them, thunderbolts and hailstones, tempestuous winds and the waves of the raging sea.

Philo also taught that the souls of the wicked were cast down into the depths of Tartarus, into blackest darkness and night, where they are surrounded by all kinds of ghostly shadows and fearful apparitions. Here they suffer a never-ending death, agonizing with present torture, and with the terror of evils to come, without relief and without hope. This sounds like the very echo of the classic fables, and brings us into the very sanctuary of Pagan belief. It is Greek, with a slightly Jewish accent.

But, not to extend this part of the inquiry too far, I shall close with citing the authority of the learned Dr. Campbell, which states very clearly the process and growth of the doctrine of retribution after death among the Jews, according to the Greek and Roman model:

"From the time of the captivity, more especially from the time of the subjection of the Jews, first to the Macedonian empire, and afterwards to the Roman, as they had a closer intercourse with Pagans, they insensibly imbibed many of their sentiments, *particularly on those points where their law was silent,* [10] and wherein by consequence they considered themselves as at greater freedom. On the subject of a future state, we find a considerable difference in the popular opinions of the Jews, in our Savior's time, from those which prevailed in the days of the ancient prophets. As both Greeks and Romans had adopted the notion that the ghosts of the departed were susceptible both of enjoyment and of suffering, they were led to suppose a sort of retribution in that state, for their merit or demerit in the present. The Jews did not adopt the pagan fables on this subject, nor did they express themselves, entirely, in the same manner; but the general train of thinking in both came pretty much to coincide." [11]

Perhaps they did not adopt the Pagan fables in every particular, but they appropriated the basis and framework of them, and invented others of their own equally gross and absurd. Le Clerc says they "borrowed so great a number of fables (*ont debite un si grand nombre de fables*), that their history, after the time of the last of the sacred historians, was scarcely more reasonable than the most fabulous histories of Paganism." And he adds, that "as they were better instructed than the Pagans, they were, therefore, more blamable for having invented so many falsehoods." [12]

They invented and borrowed, till, as Tytler says, about the time of Christ, "they had so vitiated the Law by the intermixture of heathen doctrines, and ceremonies borrowed from the Pagans," in short, "Judaism itself had become so corrupted and disguised, as to be a source of national discord and division among its votaries." [13]

These facts and testimonies are enough, I trust, to satisfy the reader of the sources from which the Jews derived the doctrine of endless punishment, and other false notions which they entertained respecting the future state. And, after this review, with what force and directness the Savior's words return upon us: "In vain they do worship me, *teaching for doctrines the commandments of men.*" Matt. xv 6-9. And we see the point of His charge against the Pharisees, that they rejected the divine commandments, that they might follow their own tradition, by which they "made the word of God of none effect" (Mark vii 9, 13); and, also, His warning to His disciples to "beware of the doctrines of the Pharisees and Sadducees." Matt. xv 6-12.

The truth is, that in the four hundred years of their intercourse with the heathen, during which they were without any divine teacher or message, Pagan philosophy and superstition had, so far as regarded the future state, completely pushed aside the Law of Moses and the Scriptures of the Old Testament, and set up in place of them their own extravagant inventions and fables respecting the invisible world. [14]

[1] Hist. Philos. Judaica. Tom. ii 703.
[2] Milman's Gibbon. Note near the beginning of chapter xxi. With regard to "paradise and hell," we think the matter overstated - there is no proof of the Babylonian origin of the last at least.
[3] Universalist Expositor, vol. for 1834, p. 423.
[4] History of Philosophy, Book iv. c. 1. See also Murdock's Mosheim, vol. I 39.

[5] Wayland's Life of Judson, vol. I 144-152.

[6] Clarke's Commentary on John ix. 2.

[7] Jewish Antiq., B. xviii., c. I 3; Jewish Wars, B. ii, c. viii. 14; B. iii., c. viii. 5.

[8] See Bush on the Resurrection, p. 253, from which I have taken these quotations.

[9] Whitby and Clarke, on John ix. 2. Schoettgen says the Jews believed in the preexistence of all souls. *Horae Hebr.,* as cited by Norton, Translation of the Gospels, ii 408.

[10] We have seen that it was silent in regard to endless punishments, and indeed all punishments after death. And it is precisely at this point where they have most freely copied from the heathen.

[11] Dissertation vi, Pt. ii, where the subject is discussed with equal candor and ability.

[12] See Jortin's Remarks, I 113. Those who have seen some of the stupid fables of the Talmud will not think this judgment of Le Clerc any too severe.

[13] Universal History, Book V, chapter iv. *Note.*

[14] The reader will find other testimonies on this important point in chap. x., sect. iii

Chapter Five - Endless Punishment Not Taught in The New Testament. Recapitulation of The Scriptural Argument.

Briefly, our argument stands, thus far, as follows: 1. If Endless Punishment be a truth, and the actual purpose of God from the beginning; and if it exerts the salutary and restraining influence claimed for it, then assuredly it ought to have been revealed at the earliest possible moment. This both Justice and Mercy required, as well as the moral and religious welfare of mankind.

We may, therefore, expect to find it announced in plainest language at the very beginning - certainly on those occasions of sin and crime which could not fail to call out some declaration of it, some threat or warning in regard to it.

But not a word do we hear of it on any such occasion. The first transgression, Cain, the Deluge, the destruction of Sodom and Gomorrah, are all passed without a single line in the sacred record respecting it. The just inference is that it cannot be true, or God would certainly have said something about it, in the course of the two thousand five hundred years of the Patriarchal Period.

2. We next examined the Law of Moses, the entire catalogue of its penalties and threatenings; but in no case did we find the least allusion to the doctrine of endless punishments, or any punishments or rewards beyond death. And we showed by the acknowledgments of the most learned critics and theolo-

gians, themselves believers in the doctrine, that it was not taught in the Law of Moses, but that the Old Testament dispensation was wholly a dispensation of temporal rewards and punishments.

This portion of the inquiry covered fifteen hundred years more, the period under the Law, during which we have no revelation from God of the awful dogma, but a studied and most remarkable silence in reference to it, if true; a silence wholly unaccountable, and which shrouds the divine character in an impenetrable darkness, and accuses beyond defense His justice and goodness.

This is the position of the question at the end of four thousand years, which brings us to the close of the Old Dispensation and the opening of the New. The inquiry now arises, Is the doctrine in review, so long concealed, brought to light in the Gospel? The very statement of the question seems almost to carry its answer with it. As if God *could* keep such a tremendous fact under cover for forty centuries, and then announce it in a revelation called preeminently good-tidings, or Gospel!

But let us see what is involved in such a supposition. If the doctrine be true, then the old patriarchs and prophets, and the chosen people of God, were all wrong some thousands of years; and the Egyptians, and Greeks, and all the heathen, were right. Those who enjoyed divine instruction were in error, while those who only had the light of nature for a guide found the truth.

But, on this supposition also, God makes a special revelation, through Christ, of what everybody knew before, Jews and Gentiles; for, as we have seen, the Jews had adopted the doctrine from the Pagans before Christ came. Heathenism had anticipated Christianity, and there was no need of a supernatural revelation of that which the Pagans had shrewdness enough to invent without any help.

Again; John says (I 17), "The Law was given by Moses, but grace and truth came by Jesus Christ." This is intended to show the superiority of Christ's mission and revelation. But which is preferable, the Law with temporal punishments, or that grace which brings in a dispensation of endless punishments? And Paul says that the Gospel is a "better covenant, established on better promises." But if it threatens this horrible judgment, not known to the Law covenant, it would be more fitting to say, it is a worse covenant established on worse threatenings. And how can Jesus be said to have "a more excellent ministry," if it involves consequences to the disobedient and unbelieving a million times more dreadful than any results of the ministry of Moses or Aaron? Heb. viii.

But let us proceed to the inquiry. Our limits will compel to utmost brevity, but we shall indicate the way with sufficient clearness.

Section I. Salvation by Christ Not from Endless Punishment.

If endless punishment really is the penalty of the Divine Law under the Gospel, and Christ came to save us from this, we may expect to have this fact announced in the most positive terms at the outset. God, so long silent, will now speak in thunder tones, and in language which all the world shall understand. Let us see if He has done so.

Luke iv. 16-22. Here we have a statement from Christ Himself, at the opening of His ministry, of what He was sent into the world for, and if the great purpose of His coming is to save men from endless misery, He will surely say so. "The spirit of the Lord is upon me, because he hath anointed me to preach the Gospel (good tidings) to the poor; he hath sent me to heal the broken-hearted, to preach deliverance to the captives, and recovering of sight to the blind, and to set at liberty them that are bruised, and to preach the acceptable year of the Lord. And he closed the book, and he gave it again to the minister (of the synagogue), and sat down."

Not a word of His being sent to save from a future endless hell; and yet He professes to tell the very object for which God did send Him! Now, if the doctrine be true, Jesus keeps up the same strange concealment which Moses maintained in the Law. He carefully enumerates all the lesser matters of His mission, but preserves a profound silence on the most momentous of all, the only thing, indeed, that brought Him into the world; and this too, just when and where He should have declared it in boldest terms.

And what is more singular still is this; reading from Isaiah (lxi 1-3), He leaves out a most important expression, viz.: "*the day of vengeance of our God.*" He reads down to these words, and then stops short in the middle of the sentence, closes the book, and sits down; as if He would say, "I have nothing to do with this; I did not come to proclaim the day of vengeance, but of deliverance." Can anything be more significant than such an omission as this? And how is it possible to explain it, if Christ did really come to reveal the day of vengeance against the wicked, and the torments of an endless hell?

But there are other passages equally significant. "God, having raised up his son Jesus, sent him to bless you," - Peter is telling the express purpose for which God raised up Jesus and sent Him into the world, and, if this purpose is to save from endless punishment, we shall certainly have it now, - "He sent him to bless you, *in turning away every one of you from his iniquities.*" Acts iii. 25, 26. And this, remember, to the very murderers of Jesus, men fresh from the hill of Calvary! If ever there was a time for revealing the doctrine of woe without end, it was here. If true, *could* Peter have omitted all allusion to it?

"He gave himself for us, that he might redeem us" - from what? endless punishment? No; "that he might redeem us from all *iniquity.*" Titus ii 11-14. "Our Lord Jesus who gave himself for our sins, that he might deliver us from"

- a future evil world? No; yet, if this be the fact, it ought to read so; but, instead of this, it reads thus: "FROM THIS PRESENT EVIL WORLD!" Gal. I 4.

Now, is not this a most marvelous thing, if Jesus really came to deliver us from a future evil world - from the endless torments of a hell which begins only after death? Plainly, if it be so, this statement of the apostle is a deliberate deception; for it not only conceals the main fact, but it substitutes something else in the place of it, as if to draw attention away from the substantial truth in the case.

Again: "Thou shalt call his name JESUS, for he shall save his people from their sins." Matt. 1. 21. Note, in passing, that the people of Jesus are sinners, since He is to save them from their sins. Commonly it is believed that saints only are His people. Note, also, that the reason given for the name Jesus, is that He shall save them from *sin,* not from the vengeance of God, or the penalty of the divine law, or the horrors of endless punishment.

These passages might be greatly multiplied, but what have been cited are enough to show that we do not find the doctrine in review revealed in the New Testament in those places, where, of all others, we had a right to expect it, if true. And if we should find it elsewhere, these passages would still be a wonder and a mystery.

But there is another fact, of great weight in this inquiry, and one worthy of all remembrance. The original words translated "save" and "salvation," if I have counted rightly, occur one hundred and fifty-seven times in the New Testament. Of these, nineteen refer to the healing of bodily infirmities; as when Jairus besought Christ to lay hands upon his daughter, "that she might be healed" - literally, "saved;" thirty-five of these refer to deliverance from danger or death, as when the mocking Jews said of Jesus, "He saved others; let him save himself."

The remaining one hundred and three examples refer to spiritual or Gospel salvation. And yet in not one of these texts is it said that Christ came to save the world, or any part of it, from endless punishment, or even from "hell." But it is said repeatedly, and emphatically, that He came expressly to save us from something quite different from this. How shall we explain this, if the doctrine be true? What shall we say of those, who, speaking by the Spirit of God in exposition of Gospel salvation, never state the case as it really is, but spend all their words on matters of comparatively trifling importance?

Section II. The New Testament Doctrine of Hell

Do we find the doctrine of endless punishment revealed in the use of the word Hell? Let the facts answer. There are three words translated "Hell" in the New Testament, *Hades* and *Tartarus,* which are Greek, and *Gehenna,* which is the Greek form of the Hebrew words *Gee* and *Hinnom,* meaning "the valley of Hinnom."

1. HADES. This word occurs eleven times, and is rendered "grave" once, and "hell" ten times. It may be profitable first to consider what one of the most accomplished orthodox scholars says in regard to it. "In my judgment," says Dr. Campbell, "it ought never in Scripture to be rendered *hell,* at least in the sense wherein that word is universally understood by Christians. In the Old Testament the corresponding word is *Sheol,* which signifies the state of the dead in general, without regard to the goodness or badness of the persons, their happiness or misery. It is very plain that neither in the Septuagint version of the Old Testament, nor in the New, does the word *hades* convey the meaning which the present English word *hell,* in the Christian usage, always conveys to our minds. The attempt to illustrate this would be unnecessary, as it is hardly now pretended by any critic that this is the acceptation of the term in the Old Testament." [1]

1st. HADES *is put for the grave, or the state of the dead.* Our translators have so rendered it in 2 Cor. xv 55. "O death, where is thy sting? O grave (*hades*), where is thy victory?" Let us look at some other passages where it is rendered "hell." "Thou wilt not leave my soul in *hell,* neither wilt thou suffer thine holy one to see corruption." "He spake of the resurrection of Christ, that his soul was not left in *hell,* neither did his flesh see corruption." Acts ii 27, 31. Was the soul of Christ ever in hell, in the orthodox sense of the word, as a place of endless torment? But the sacred writer himself explains the word, when he says he is speaking of the *resurrection* of Christ, that is, from the grave, or the dead.

"And I looked, and behold a pale horse; and his name that sat on him was death, and *hell* followed him." Rev. vi 8. There is no necessary connection between death and a place of endless punishment, as all men die, good or bad; but there is a connection between death and the grave, or the state of the dead; and there is a propriety in representing the last as following the first. "And death and hell delivered up the dead which were in them." Rev. xx. 13. This is the reverse of what is usually taught and believed of hell; for the leading idea is that it will *not* give up those who are in it. Surely the hell the Revelator speaks of is not a place of *endless* torments. This is further confirmed by the next verse, where it is said, "death and *hell* were cast into the lake of fire," that is, utterly destroyed. Of course, then, this hell cannot be a place of endless woe, since it is not itself endless.

These passages, which are without point or meaning in the common view of hell, are full of significance when we give to *hades,* or *hell,* its true sense. For we know that the grave (*hades*) will deliver up its dead, and that death and the grave will be destroyed in the resurrection, when death shall be swallowed up in the victory of immortal life. Then with a meaning it will be said, "O grave (*hades, hell*), where is thy victory?" for then will be fulfilled the saying, "O grave (*hades, hell*), I will be thy destruction." Hosea xiii. 14.

2d. HADES *is also used in a figurative sense to represent a state of degradation, calamity, or suffering, arising from any cause whatever.*

"And thou, Capernaum, which art exalted unto heaven, shalt be brought down to hell" (*hades*). Matt. xi 23. The parallel passage is in Luke, x. 15. No one supposes that the city of Capernaum went down to a place of endless woe. The word *hell* here, as Dr. Clarke says, is a figure to set forth "the state of utmost woe, and ruin, and desolation, to which these impenitent cities should be reduced. This prediction of our Lord was literally fulfilled." Bp. Pearce says, "It means, thou shalt be quite ruined and destroyed." So also Hammond, Beausobre, Bloomfield, and others. The last named says it is a "hyberbolical expression, figuratively representing the depth of adversity."

The parable of the rich man and Lazarus furnishes another example. "And in hell (*hades*) he lifted up his eyes, being in torment." It will be remembered that the Jews had borrowed their ideas of torment in a future state from the heathen, and of course they were obliged to borrow their terms to express this. Accordingly, after the manner of the Greeks, *Hades,* or the place of departed spirits, is represented as receiving all, as *Sheol* did, good and bad; but we have also the additional idea of separate apartments or districts, divided by a great gulf or river; on one side of which the blessed are located, and on the other side the damned, near enough to see each other, and converse together, as in the case of Abraham and the rich man.

It must also be remembered that this is only a parable, and not a real history; for, as Dr. Whitby affirms, "we find this very parable in the *Gemara Babylonicum.*" The story was not new, then, not original with Christ, but known among the Jews before He repeated it. He borrowed the parable from them, and employed it to show the judgment which awaited them. He represented the spiritual favors and privileges of the Jews by the wealth and luxury of the rich man, and the spiritual poverty of the Gentiles by the beggary and infirmity of Lazarus; and while the former would be deprived of their privileges and punished for their wickedness, the latter would enjoy the blessings of truth and faith.

The question may arise, "If Christ employed the language used by the Jews to express the torments of hell after death, did He not virtually sanction the doctrine?"

If so, then He sanctioned their views as set out in this parable, which, as we have already shown, they borrowed from the heathen. He puts Himself on a level with the Pagan poets, and teaches a heaven and hell in Hades, divided by a great gulf, torments by flame, conversational intercourse between the blessed and the damned, &c.

Now no one believes in such a hell as this. A material hell of fire, and torments by flame, have been long ago abandoned. And the Savior cannot be understood as believing or teaching future torments, by using this parable, any more than He can be supposed to believe and teach the existence of Beelzebub, the Philistine god of flies (or filth), when He alludes to him, and uses his name as if he were a real being. See Matt. x. 25; xii 24.

So He says (Matt. vi 24), "Ye cannot serve God and mammon." "Mammon" is the name of the god of riches; but surely no one would pretend that Christ, by speaking of serving him, sanctioned the doctrine that he was really a god. And yet He speaks of his service in the same connection, and in the same language, with that of the true God; showing the latitude with which these comparisons and figures are used, without sanctioning the errors on which they are founded. He takes their own language and opinions in both cases, without believing or approving, in order to teach and warn them.

Dr. Macknight (Scotch Presbyterian) has spoken well on this point. "It must be acknowledged," he says, "that our Lord's descriptions (in this parable) are not drawn from the writings of the Old Testament, but have a remarkable affinity to the descriptions which the Grecian poets have given. They, as well as our Lord, represent the abodes of the blessed as lying contiguous to the region of the damned, and separated only by a great impassable river, or deep gulf, in such sort that the ghosts could talk to one another from its opposite banks. The parable says the souls of wicked men are tormented in flames; the Grecian mythologists tell us they lie in Phlegethon, the river of fire, where they suffer torments," &c. Then he adds, "If from these resemblances it is thought the parable is formed on the Grecian mythology, *it will not at all follow that our Lord approved of what the common people thought or spake concerning those matters,* agreeably to the notions of the Greeks. In parabolical discourses, provided the doctrines inculcated are strictly true, the terms in which they are inculcated may be such as are most familiar to the ears of the vulgar, and the images made use of such as they are best acquainted with." *Whittemore's Notes.*

The sum of the matter is, that Christ takes up a parable or story current among the Jews, and, without approving the heathen opinions on which it was founded, uses it to show that the Gentiles (Lazarus) would be received into the Gospel kingdom with Abraham and Isaac, while the Jews (the rich man) would be thrust out into darkness and desolation. And this judgment he represents by the figure of casting into hell, as He had described the destruction of Capernaum by saying it would be "thrust down to hell."

A perfect commentary on the parable is found in such passages as these: "The kingdom of God shall be taken from you, and given to a nation bringing forth the fruits thereof." Matt xxi 43. "There shall be weeping and gnashing of teeth, when ye see many coming from the east and from the west, from the north and from the south, and sitting with Abraham and Isaac and Jacob in the kingdom of God, while you yourselves are thrust out." Matt. viii. 11, compared with Luke xiii. 28, 29. "It was necessary that the word of God should first have been spoken to you; but, seeing ye put it from you, and judge (show) yourselves unworthy of everlasting life, lo, we turn to the Gentiles." Acts xiii. 46.

2. TARTARUS. This word occurs only once, and then in a participial form, in 2 Peter ii 4. "If God spared not the angels that sinned, but cast them down to hell, &c. *Tartarosas.* This is of the same character with the parable just considered, Tartarus being the place of torment in *Hades,* where the rich man was supposed to be. Bloomfield says that "Tartarus here is derived from the

59

heathen, and chains of darkness from the Jewish mythology;" and adds "it is an expression truly Aeschylean," that is, dramatic, not literally true, a figure of something else.

It cannot be supposed that the divine apostle believed in the heathen hell or Tartarus, of which we have given some account in Chapter iii., and which the heathen themselves confess is a mere fable, an invention of legislators and poets. His use of the word does not prove his belief of the doctrine of torments after death, any more than Jude's mention of the dispute between Michael and the devil about the body of Moses, makes him responsible for the truth of that idle and ridiculous fable of the Jews. It might as well be argued that he believed the angels or messengers were bound in literal "chains of darkness," as that he believed they were literally cast into Tartarus or the heathen hell. Both expressions are figures to represent the desolation or destruction into which they were brought by their disobedience.

This is not the place to enter into the question of who are meant by the angels, or to give an exposition of the passage. Whether men or spirits, the word "hell" here furnishes no proof of their endless punishment - and this is all we are concerned with in the present inquiry.

3. GEHENNA. This word occurs twelve times in the New Testament, and is always translated "hell." But as the Evangelists repeat the same discourses, the Savior did not really use it more than six or seven times in all His ministry. The following are the texts: Matt. V 22, 29, 30, x. 28, xviii. 9, xxiii. 15, 33; Mark ix. 43, 45, 47; Luke xii 5; James iii. 6. By consulting these passages the reader will see how many of them are simply repetitions, and how very few times this word is used, on which, nevertheless, more reliance is placed than on all others, to prove that "hell" is a place of endless torment.

The following from Schleusner, a distinguished lexicographer and critic, will show the origin of the word, and indicate its scriptural usage: "*Gehenna,* originally a Hebrew word, which signifies *valley of Hinnom.* Here the Jews placed that brazen image of Moloch. It is said, on the authority of the ancient Rabbins, that to this image the idolatrous Jews were wont not only to sacrifice doves, pigeons, lambs, &c., but even to offer their own children. In the prophecies of Jeremiah (vii 31), this valley is called *Tophet,* from *Toph,* a drum; because they beat a drum during these horrible rites, lest the cries and shrieks of the infants who were burned should be heard by the assembly. At length these nefarious practices were abolished by Josiah, and the Jews brought back to the pure worship of God. 2 Kings xxiii. After this they held the place in such abomination that they cast into it all kinds of filth, and the carcasses of beasts, and the unburied bodies of criminals who had been executed. Continual fires were necessary in order to consume these, lest the putrefaction should infect the air; and there were always worms feeding on the remaining relics. *Hence it came, that any severe punishment, especially an infamous kind of death, was described by the word Gehenna,* or hell." [2]

It is proper to add that Schleusner also says that it was used to represent the future torments of the wicked, and attempts to show it by quoting the texts given above. But this, as the reader will see, is assuming the whole question; it is taking for granted the thing to be proved.

In Jeremiah xix., it seems to be used as a comparative symbol of the desolation of Jerusalem by the Chaldeans, or, as Dr. Clarke thinks, by the Romans. The Lord says to the prophet, "Go forth into the valley of the Son of Hinnom (*Gehenna, hell*); and proclaim there the words that I shall tell thee...I will even make this city as Tophet (or Gehenna); and the houses of Jerusalem and the kings of Judah shall be defiled as the place of Tophet," &c. Here *Tophet*, or *Gehenna*, is employed in the way of comparison to set forth the utter overthrow of Jerusalem; as we say of a place, "It is barren as a desert," "It is silent as the grave," &c.

Isaiah says, "They shall go forth, and look upon the carcasses of the men that have transgressed against me; for their worm shall not die, neither shall their fire be quenched; and they shall be an abhorring unto all flesh." lxvi 23, 24. Here the unquenchable fire and the undying worm of *Gehenna*, or *hell*, are used as figures of judgment to happen on the earth, where there are carcasses, new moons, sabbaths, &c. *Gehenna*, with its accompaniments, was an object of utmost loathing to the Jew, and came to be employed as a symbol of any great judgment or woe.

We say of a great military or political overthrow, "It was a Waterloo defeat." So the Jews described a great desolation by a like use of the word Gehenna - "It was a Gehenna judgment;" that is, a very terrible and destructive judgment.

In Matt. V 29, 30, there is mention of the "whole body cast into hell." No one supposes the *body* is literally cast into a hell in the future state. The severity of the judgments falling on those who would not give up their sins, is represented by *Gehenna*, which, as Schleusner says, was "a word in common use to describe any severe punishment, especially an infamous kind of death." These wicked people should perish in a manner as infamous as that of criminals, whose bodies, after execution, were cast into Gehenna (hell), and burned with the bodies of beasts and the offal of the city.

The same thought is expressed in Matt. xxiii. 33, where "the damnation of hell" is a symbol of the tremendous judgments coming upon that guilty nation, when inquisition would be made for "all the righteous blood shed upon the earth, from the blood of righteous Abel unto the blood of Zacharias, son of Barachias, slain between the temple and the altar." Vs. 34-39.

Mark ix. 33, 45, 47, are repetitions of Matt. V 29, 30, with the addition of "the undying worm and the unquenchable fire," which is a repetition of Isaiah lxvi 24. There is nothing in the passage to show that the Savior used these phrases in any sense different from that of the prophet; who, as we have seen, employs them to represent judgments on the earth, where, "they shall go forth to look on the carcasses of the men who have transgressed against me...for they shall bury in Tophet (the place of sacrifice in Gehenna or hell) till there is no place;...and the days shall come that it shall no more be called Tophet, nor the valley of the Son of Hinnom (the Hebrew for Gehenna or hell), but the valley of Slaughter." Jer. vii 19; Isa. lxvi 24.

"Fear not them which kill the body, but are not able to kill the soul; but rather fear him which is able to destroy both soul and body in hell." Matt. x. 28. Luke says, "Fear him, which, after he hath killed, hath power to cast into hell." xii 5.

Here is a mixed reference, figurative and literal, to the valley of Hinnom, Gehenna, hell. There is a literal allusion to casting the dead bodies of criminals into the valley, to be burned in the perpetual or unquenchable fire kept up there for this purpose; but the association of soul and body in the same destruction indicates the figurative use to represent entire extinction of being, or annihilation.

Isaiah employs the phrase in a similar way. "The Lord shall kindle a burning like the burning of a fire...and it shall burn and devour his thorns and his briers in one day; and shall consume the glory of his forest, and of his fruitful field, *both soul and body.*" x. 16-18. Dr. Clarke says this is "a proverbial expression," signifying that they should be "entirely and altogether consumed." So Christ represents God as able to destroy the wicked and apostate, "soul and body in Gehenna," the word familiarly used to express any great judgment or calamity. [3]

But the Savior is not to be understood as teaching that God *will* annihilate soul and body, because He said He was able to do it, any more than He is to be understood as teaching that out of stones God would raise up children to Abraham, because He said He was able to. Matt. iiI 9. And, moreover, He tells them in the very next words *not* to fear, because God watched over them, numbering the hairs of their head even, in His special keeping of them, and would surely protect them so long as they were faithful to Him and His truth.

The method of argument seems to be the same as that pursued with the Pharisees, when they complained of His keeping company with publicans and sinners. Matt. ix. "I am not come to call the righteous, but sinners to repentance." If you are righteous, as you pretend, that is good reason why I should not keep company with you, for I came to save sinners. But He did not allow that they *were* righteous. He only admitted their premises for the time, in order to show the absurdity of their reasoning.

So, here, He says: If you are moved by the selfish consideration of fear to abandon the Gospel in order to save your lives (as Peter was afterward tempted to do), then, to be consistent, you ought to fear the power which can do you most injury. And this surely is God, who can bring destruction and death, not only on the body, but on the soul also, and that amid the most terrible of judgments. And to picture the dreadfulness of this destruction more vividly to their minds, He uses the well-known symbol of Gehenna, or the valley of Hinnom, the synonym of all that was horrible in the mind of a Jew. [4]

Then, in the next words, He proceeds to tell them that really they had no cause to fear either God or men. So long as they did their duty, God, who provided for the sparrow (vs. 29), and numbered the hairs of their heads, in the watchfulness of His love (vs. 30), would surely protect them. And, then, as if to convince them that what He had said was only a supposition, and not a fact, He says: "FEAR YE NOT, THEREFORE, ye are of more value than many sparrows." (vs. 31.)

In the two passages following, Gehenna seems to be employed as a figure or symbol of moral corruption.

James says of the tongue, "It defileth the whole body, and setteth on fire the course of nature; and it is set on fire of hell" (*Gehenna*). iii. 6. Here Gehenna, that place of filth and corruption and perpetual fires, is made a fitting emblem of the foul passions and corrupt appetites, set on fire by a foul and seductive tongue, which inflames in turn, to the defilement of the whole body.

So, in Matt. xxiii. 15, 27, Gehenna or hell, and the whited sepulcher, "full of dead men's bones, and all uncleanness," are fearful symbols of the moral foulness of the "Scribes, Pharisees, and hypocrites," whom the Savior was addressing. "Two-fold more the child of hell," signifying that they made their converts two-fold more corrupt than themselves.

The word Gehenna, or hell, then, in the New Testament is used as a symbol of anything that was foul and repulsive; but especially as a figure of dreadful and destructive judgments.

And, now, let us consider some of the facts connected with this word *Gehenna.* They are the more important because this word is specially relied upon as teaching the doctrine of endless torments, the doctrine of hell, as popularly believed. Whatever other forms of speech may be employed to express the thought, this is surely one of the terms clearly declarative of future endless punishment.

Admitting this statement for a moment, let us see what follows. If this is *the* word by which the tremendous fact is to be revealed, we shall have it notified to us in a fitting manner. We know with what solemn preparations, and awful accompaniments, the Law was introduced at Sinai; and we may certainly expect this doctrine will be announced with a solemnity and awfulness corresponding to its infinitely greater importance, and which shall concentrate upon it the attention of all the world. Neither the patriarchs, nor Moses, nor the prophets, have uttered a word on the subject; but now a new teacher is come from God, and he is to make known the dreadful doctrine; and the words he selects for this purpose will be employed with a power of emphasis, with a marked distinction, which will shut out all possibility of mistake.

Let us see if it be so. The first time Christ uses the word *Gehenna* is in Matt. V 22, 29, 30. But not a word of preparation or notice that now, for the first time, the terrible dogma is announced on divine authority. He speaks as calmly as if He were wholly unconscious of the burthen of such a revelation; and the people seem equally unmoved under the awful declaration. And what is singular, it is not presented by itself, in a positive form, unmixed with anything else, as its importance most surely demanded; but is slipped in merely as a comparative illustration, among other judgments, of the greater moral demands of the Gospel, and the strictness with which it enforced obedience.

They, the Jews, had said, "Whosoever shall kill, shall be in danger of the judgment;" but Christ says, whosoever is angry with his brother without cause, is in danger of a punishment equal to that of the judgment (the inferior court of seven judges); and whosoever shall say to his brother, Raca (a term of contempt, shallow-brain or blockhead), shall be in danger of a punishment equal to that inflicted by the council (the superior court of seventy judges, which took cognizance of capital crimes); but whosoever shall say, "Thou fool, shall be in danger of hell-fire," or of a punishment equal in severity to the fire of Gehenna.

Now, if Christ used the term *Gehenna* to reveal endless woe, and that for the first time, would He not have said this, and fixed forever the meaning of the word? And yet not the slightest intimation do we have of any such new and awful meaning. The Jews were familiar with it, and used it constantly to symbolize any great punishment or judgment coming on the earth; and they must of course suppose He used it as they did, since He gave them no notice to the contrary. If, therefore, He did give it the new signification of endless punishment after death, they could not understand Him, and He failed of His purpose for want of such explanation as they, and we, had a right to expect.

But there is another consideration deserving notice. The difference between the sinfulness of saying Raca or Blockhead, and Fool, is hardly great enough to warrant such a difference in punishment as is involved in the supposition. Townsend justly says, to imagine that Christ, for such a slight distinction as Raca and Thou fool, "would instantly pass from such a sentence as the Jewish Sanhedrim would pronounce, to the awful doom of eternal punishment in hell-fire, is what cannot be reconciled to any rational rule of faith, or known measure of justice." There is no proportion between the slight difference in guilt and the tremendous, infinite difference in punishment. But if the comparison is between penalties symbolized by stoning to death, inflicted by the Sanhedrim council, and burning alive in Gehenna, then there *is* proportion, some relation of parts; because the difference between death by stoning and death by burning is not certainly very great; but the difference between death by stoning and endless torment is infinite.

It is impossible, therefore, to believe that Christ, in this first use of *Gehenna,* intended to reveal the doctrine, without an accusation against His fidelity and justice.

But let us note other facts equally pertinent.

1. Though *Gehenna* occurs twelve times, the Savior actually used it only on four or five different occasions, the rest being only repetitions. If this is *the* word, and the revelation of this terrible doctrine is in it, how is it possible that Christ, in a ministry of three years, should use it only four times? Was He faithful to the souls committed to His charge?

2. The Savior and James are the only persons in all the New Testament who use the word. John Baptist, who preached to the most wicked of men, did not

use it once. Paul wrote *fourteen epistles,* and yet never once mentions it. Peter does not name it, nor Jude; and John, who wrote the gospel, three epistles, and the Book of Revelations, never employs it in a single instance. Now if *Gehenna* or *hell* really reveals the terrible fact of endless woe, how *can* we account for this strange silence? How is it possible, if they knew its meaning, and believed it a part of Christ's teaching, that they should not have used it a hundred or a thousand times, instead of never using it at all; especially when we consider the infinite interests involved?

3. The Book of Acts contains the record of the apostolic preaching, and the history of the first planting of the Church among the Jews and Gentiles, and embraces a period of *thirty years* from the ascension of Christ. In all this history, in all this preaching of the disciples and apostles of Jesus, there is no mention of *Gehenna.* In thirty years of missionary effort, these men of God, addressing people of all characters and nations, never, under any circumstances, threaten them with the torments of *Gehenna,* or allude to it in the most distant manner! In the face of such a fact as this, can any man believe that *Gehenna* signifies endless punishment, and that this is a part of divine revelation, a part of the Gospel message to the world?

These considerations show how impossible it is to establish the doctrine in review on the word *Gehenna.* All the facts are against the supposition that the term was used by Christ or His disciples in the sense of future endless punishment. There is not the least hint of any such meaning attached to it, nor the slightest preparatory notice that any such new revelation was to be looked for in this old familiar word.

We have now passed in review, as far as our limits will permit, the New Testament doctrine of *Hell,* and we have not, surely, found it to be the doctrine of endless punishment, but something very wide from this. Let us now turn to other phraseology supposed to embody this thought, and to establish it as a doctrine of divine revelation.

Section III. "Unquenchable Fire" and "The Worm That Dieth Not."

These expressions are regarded as among the most terrible to be found in the Scriptures; and by a large portion of Christian believers are considered as decisive of the endless duration of the punishment of the wicked.

The phrase "unquenchable fire," or "the fire that shall not be quenched," occurs in the following passages of the New Testament: Matt. iii. 12, Luke iii. 17, Mark ix. 43, 44, 45, 46, 48. In the passages from Mark it is found in connection with the phrase "the worm that dieth not." The repetitions of the same expression are obvious, the terms being thrice repeated (of the eye, the hand, the foot) simply for emphasis.

The origin of the phraseology in the desecration of the valley of Hinnom, or hell, making it a place for the deposit and burning of dead bodies and offal, has already been given in the previous section. The Savior borrows it from the prophet Isaiah; and it is important to observe that He uses the phrase "unquenchable fire" only on two occasions, and the phrase "the worm that dieth not" only on one occasion, that recorded by Mark. [5] If the language implies as much as is affirmed, this is strange enough for a ministry of three entire years.

Our first inquiry is into the Scripture usage of the language, and, this ascertained, we shall be able to decide how much it has to do with the question of endless punishment. "If ye will not hearken unto me...then will I kindle a fire in the gates of Jerusalem, and it shall devour the palaces of Jerusalem, *and it shall not be quenched."* Jer. xvii 27. This unquenchable fire certainly belonged to this world, and had relation to the destruction of the gates and palaces of Jerusalem.

"Therefore, thus saith the Lord God: Behold mine anger and my fury shall be poured out upon this place, upon man, and upon beast, and upon the trees of the field, and upon the fruit of the ground, and it shall burn, and shall not be quenched." Jer. vii 20. No one, I suppose, would argue that the beasts of the field, and the fruits of the ground, were made endlessly miserable because it is said the anger and the fury of God were poured out upon them in fire unquenchable. Nothing can show more plainly that the expression is a figure, representing the severity of the divine judgments, in this case, on "the cities of Judah and Jerusalem."

The prophet Isaiah describes the desolation of Idumea in the following language: "The streams thereof shall be turned into pitch, and the dust thereof into brimstone, and the land thereof shall become burning pitch. *It shall not be quenched night nor day; the smoke thereof shall go up forever."* xxxiv. 5-10. This strong language is employed to set forth the destruction of a petty tribe, occupying a territory ten or fifteen miles square; and furnishes an important illustration of the elasticity with which the phrases in review are used as symbols of temporal judgments.

One more example: The overthrow of the Jews, and the laying waste of Judea, by Nebuchadnezzar and the Chaldeans, is predicted by Ezekiel in the terms following: "I will kindle a fire in thee, and it shall devour every green tree in thee, and every dry tree; *the flaming flame shall not be quenched,* and all faces from north to south shall be burned therein. And all flesh shall see that I the Lord have kindled it: *it shall not be quenched."* xx. 47, 48. See, also, Isa. I 31; Jer. iv. 4, xxxi 12; Amos V 6.

These passages are sufficient to show that the sacred writers used the phrases in review as figures of God's judgments in the earth, of the calamities which He sent upon wicked nations, through the agency of war, famine and desolation. In not one of the texts cited is the language employed as a figure of any judgments or sufferings but such as belong to time and earth; and these are all the passages in the Old Testament in which it occurs, with the exception of Isaiah lxvi 23, 24, which has been considered under the head of *Gehenna.*

Now, if the Savior used the same phraseology used by the prophets and the Jews, He would undoubtedly employ it in the same sense, if He wished or expected them to understand Him. The prophets had employed these expressions, and the people were familiar with the use of them, as symbols of terrible judgments and punishments sent upon the guilty nations, falling on the transgressors in this life. Their Scriptures never use them in any other sense, and the significance of the language was in regard to the severity, and not the duration, of the punishment. Hence, as Hammond, an excellent commentator of the English church, says, "unquenchable fire" is simply "a fire never quenched till it has done its work," or, in other words, a thoroughly destructive fire.

Dr. Clarke says, on Matt. iii. 12: "He will burn up the chaff, that is, *the disobedient and rebellious Jews,* with unquenchable fire, *that cannot be extinguished by man."* Le Clerc says: "By these words is signified the utter destruction of the Jews;" and Bp. Pearce remarks: "In this whole verse the destruction of the Jewish state is expressed in the terms of the husbandman." [See Paige's *Selections.*] These eminent orthodox writers understand the scriptural usage of the language, and show us that the judgments symbolized by it are not endless in duration, nor located beyond the earth. It is plain, therefore, that the Savior employed the phrases in question in the same sense in which the prophets had employed them, the sense which the people attached to them; that of a terrible and desolating judgment, without any reference to the time of its continuance. The idea of endlessness seems never to have been thought of in connection with the phraseology; nor duration of any length, indeed, but only the intensity and destructiveness of the punishment or judgment.

To illustrate the subject still further, and to show how utterly groundless is the assumption that these expressions necessarily imply endless duration, let us call in the testimony of some Greek authors, who certainly have a right to know the meaning of their own language.

1. *Strabo,* the celebrated geographer, speaking of the Parthenon, a temple in Athens, says: "In this was the inextinguishable or unquenchable lamp" (*asbestos,* the very word used in Mark iii. 12, Luke iii. 17, and Mark ix. 43). Of course, all it means is that the lamp was kept constantly or regularly burning during the period alluded to, though extinguished or quenched ages ago.

2. *Homer* uses the phrase *asbestos gelos,* "unquenchable laughter." But we can hardly suppose they are laughing now, and will laugh to all eternity.

3. *Plutarch,* the well-known author of the biographies familiarly known as "Plutarch's Lives," calls the sacred fire of the temple "unquenchable fire" (*pur asbeston,* the exact expression of Jesus), though he says in the very next sentence it had sometimes gone out.

4. *Josephus,* speaking of a festival of the Jews, says that every one brought fuel for the fire of the altar, which "continued *always unquenchable,"* (*asbeston aei*). Here we have a union of the word supposed to mean specially endless, when in the form of *aionios,* with the word "unquenchable," and yet

both together do not convey the idea of duration without end; for the fire of which Josephus speaks had actually gone out, and the altar been destroyed, at the time he wrote! And still he calls the fire "always unquenchable."

5. *Eusebius,* the father of ecclesiastical history, describing the martyrdom of several Christians at Alexandria, says: "They were carried on camels through the city, and in this elevated position were scourged, and finally consumed or burned in *unquenchable fire*" (*puri asbesto*). [6] Here, again, we have the very phrase employed by our Lord, and applied to a literal fire, which, of course, was quenched in the short space of one hour, probably, or two hours at the longest. All that is implied is, that it burned till it had consumed the victims.

These authors, writing in their own tongue, must have known the value and import of the phrase "unquenchable fire;" and it is as clear as demonstration can make it that they did not use it to mean endless. And shall any one, however learned, presume to understand Greek better than the Greeks themselves?

Eusebius has given us a perfect illustration of the scriptural usage and just definition of the term, as relating to intensity and destructive severity, rather than to length of time. And the Savior, in Mark ix., employs it as a figure of the terrible judgment which was to destroy the enemies and the false professors of the Gospel, without any more reference to duration than Eusebius had when speaking of the unquenchable fire that consumed the bodies of the martyrs.

The following facts, then, are established. 1. The whole Old Testament usage of the language in review is against the meaning of endless, as the passages cited and referred to fully show. 2. The Greek writers quoted above did not use it to signify *endless;* which gives us both scriptural and classical usage against it. 3. There is not one particle of proof to show that the Savior used it in the sense of *endless,* or in any other sense than that of the prophets, viz., a figure or symbol of great temporal judgments.

We do not yet, therefore, find the doctrine of endless punishment revealed in the New Testament, nor in any way sanctioned by the authority or language of the blessed Savior. There is one other class of phrases, or words, which will require attention; and this will close the inquiry on this head.

Section IV. The Words Eternal, Everlasting, Forever, Etc.

These words are regarded by many as settling the question of the endless duration of punishment - with how little reason the facts will show. It is remarkable that, though the original words rendered "everlasting," "eternal," &c. (*aion* and *aionios*), occur together *one hundred and seventy-nine* times in the New Testament, they are used only *twelve* times in connection with punishment. "Everlasting fire" occurs three times, and "everlasting punishment" once, "everlasting destruction" once, and "eternal damnation" once! Matt.

xviii. 8, xxv 41, 46; 2 Thess. I 9; Mark iii. 29. The other texts are Heb. vi 2; 2 Pet. ii 17; Jude 7, 13. Surely, if the words everlasting and eternal mean strictly endless by their own inherent force, this is very singular. The Gospel a special revelation of endless punishment, and yet the words expressing this awful fact, applied to it only nine times out of a usage of one hundred and seventy-nine examples! [7]

Let us now attend to the definition and usage of the words by lexicographers, and classical and scriptural writers, that we may be able to judge of its value in the present discussion.

1. *Lexicographers and Critics.* Schleusner, whose exact learning makes his authority of great weight, defines the noun *aion,* thus: "Any space of time, whether longer or shorter, past, present, or future, to be determined by the persons or things spoken of, and the scope of the subject - the life or age of man; any space in which we measure human life, from birth to death."

Donnegan. "*Aion,* time; a space of time; life time and life; the ordinary period of man's life, the age of man; man's estate; a long period of time; eternity. *Aionios,* of long duration; eternal, lasting, permanent."

Schrevelius. "*Aion,* an age, a long period of time; indefinite duration; time, whether longer or shorter, past, present or future; life, the life of man. *Aionios,* of long duration, lasting, sometimes everlasting, sometimes lasting through life."

Authorities might be multiplied to any extent, but these are sufficient to show that the radical meaning of the Greek words translated "everlasting," "forever," &c., is *not endless,* but simply *indefinite time,* longer or shorter, past or future; and that they take their force as to duration from the subjects or persons to which they are applied. If they mean strictly endless in any case, it is not because that idea is in the words *aionios, aion,* "everlasting," "forever;" but because the being or subject qualified demands it, or is, of itself, necessarily endless.

Hence Dr. Macknight, Presbyterian, says: "These words, being ambiguous, are always to be understood according to the nature and circumstances of the things to which they are applied." And though he claims the words in support of endless punishment, yet he frankly adds: "At the same time, I must be so candid as to acknowledge, that the use of these terms *forever, eternal,* and *everlasting,* in other passages of Scripture, shows that they who understand the words in a limited sense when applied to punishment, put no forced interpretation on them." [8]

2. *Usage of Greek Authors.* The Greek writers constantly employ these words in a way to exclude the idea of endless, and to illustrate the meaning of indefinite time, the duration to be determined by the general scope of the subject.

Plato has the phrase "eternal (*aionios*) drunkenness;" but one can hardly believe he meant *endless* drunkenness.

Eusebius, one of the early Christian writers, speaking of the Phoenician philosophy as presented by Sanchoniathon, says of the darkness and chaos which preceded creation: "They continued for a *long eternity*" - (*dia polun aiona*). Here the word is qualified by long, showing that eternity means simply age or time indefinite, long or short.

"And these they called *aionios,* eternal, hearing that they had performed the sacred rites for *three entire generations." In Solom. Parab.* This eternity was three generations long, or about one hundred years. "Alter not the eternal boundaries." If "eternal" implied endless, they could not be altered.

These examples might be multiplied, but my purpose is only to furnish the reader with a sufficient number to enable him to judge of the usage among the Greeks themselves, who, of course, will be allowed to understand the signification of words in their own language. I shall cite one more authority from classic usage, because his definition has been claimed as decisive of the meaning "endless," as the radical idea of *aion,* from which comes *aionios,* "everlasting," "forever," &c.

"According to *Aristotle,* and a higher authority need not be sought, *aion* is compounded of *aei, always,* and *on, being;* that is, *always existing,..interminable, incessant, and immeasurable duration."* Clarke on Gen. xxi 33. Others also compel Aristotle into the same service.

Now, a single passage *from the same work* in which Aristotle is represented as defining *aion* to mean radically and strictly endless, duration without end, will show the uncertainty of such criticism, and the folly of attempting to press the great philosopher into the support of endless punishment. The passage referred to (*De Mundo*), has this expression: "from one interminable eternity to another eternity" - *ex aionos atermonos eis eteron aiona.*

Now, if Aristotle intended to define *aion* as signifying strictly *endless,* as Dr. Clarke affirms, why did he add another word to increase the force of it? Where the need or sense of saying from one *interminable eternity* to another? And even with this addition he does not convey the idea of duration without limit or end; otherwise there could not be another such period, which the sentence affirms! Plainly he uses the words in the ordinary sense, meaning by them only indefinite time, endless or limited, as the nature of the subject may require. And even when joined with the adjective *atermonos,* "without limit or termination," it is not to be taken too literally, as signifying a strict eternity.

In a poem ascribed to Errina Lesbia there is a similar use of the adjective "greatest" in connection with aion - "the greatest eternity that overturns all things," &c., *ho megistos aion.* The greatest eternity implies a less one; and is demonstrative proof that the noun *aion* and the adjective *aionios* convey the idea not of strictly endless duration, but only of duration indefinitely continued.

Philo and *Josephus* wrote in Greek, though Jews by birth. The former uses the very phrase found in Matt. xxv 46, "everlasting punishment" - *kolasis aionios* - as follows: - Speaking of the manner in which certain persons retaliate an injury, he designates it as "a deep hatred and *everlasting punishment.*"

Of course the everlasting punishment in this case is inflicted by men in this life, and cannot, therefore, last much above "three-score years and ten."

Josephus employs the word in such phrases as these: "the *everlasting* name of the patriarchs;" "the *everlasting* glory of the Jewish nation," which ended two thousand years ago; "the *everlasting* reputation" of Herod; "the *everlasting* worship" in the temple, which also ceased nearly eighteen hundred years ago; "the everlasting imprisonment" to which John, the tyrant, was condemned by the Romans, though it could not continue but a few years at most. [9]

These Jewish-Greek authors were contemporary with the New Testament authors, and are therefore good authority for the usage and meaning of the words in review, embracing both the Greek and Jewish elements. Philo and Josephus, Matthew and Luke, allowing for the difference in education, stood in the same relation to the Greek language, and the Jewish usage of it, and what may be affirmed of one may be affirmed with equal force of the others. And, surely, nothing is more obvious than that the first named did not understand the words *aion* and *aionios* as meaning anything more than indefinite time.

Another decisive fact is this: The *Sibylline Oracles, Clemens Alexandrinus, Origen,* and others of the Christian Fathers, who are acknowledged believers and teachers of the final restoration, often use the phrases "everlasting fire," "everlasting punishment," &c., in regard to the wicked. Nothing can more conclusively show that the expressions are not to be taken in the sense of endless; for, though they believed in everlasting punishment, they also believed it would end in the restoration of those who suffered.

3. *Scripture Usage.* The Scripture usage will be found in perfect harmony with the foregoing facts. The Hebrew word, which is the equivalent of the Greek, is thus used: "I will give thee the land of Canaan for an *everlasting* possession." Gen. xvii 8. And in verse 12, the covenant of circumcision is called "an everlasting covenant." And yet the Jews were driven from the land of Canaan, and the covenant of circumcision was abolished, eighteen hundred years ago! So the priesthood of Aaron is called "an everlasting priesthood," and yet it was put aside by God's authority, and the priesthood of Christ set up in its place. Exod. xl. 15.

Now, did Jehovah use this word "everlasting" to mean endless? If He did, then He has broken His promise to the Jews in three several instances; or, if not this, the priesthood of Christ is an imposture, and the old Covenant of the Law is still in force! See, also, Levit. xvi 34, xxv 46; Exod. xxi 6.

Jonah ii 1-6, is another illustration, where "forever" lasted *only three days and three nights!* showing the folly of arguing for the endlessness of punishment on the strength of such elastic words as these. The punishment of Jonah is described by the term "forever," though it lasted only seventy-two hours; and there is no more reason for supposing the term to mean endless in other cases, when applied to punishment, than here. There is no more authority for saying the "everlasting punishment" of Matt. xxv 46, is endless, than for saying the "forever" punishment of Jonah, or the "everlasting priesthood" of Exod. xl. 15, is endless.

The word may sometimes be used to signify a strict eternity; but it takes its force in such cases from the subject or person to whom it is applied. For example, in the expression "everlasting God," everlasting means endless, because God is immortal, not by any force of its own. The word "everlasting" borrows its endlessness from God, not God from "everlasting."

So, in all cases, the adjective is modified by the noun. A strong horse, a strong mind, a strong chain, strong drink, strong language - in each one of these phrases "strong" has a different meaning, according to the nature of the subject or noun. So a wise man, a wise God - in the last case the word "wise" means infinite wisdom, but not in the first; and the meaning of infinite is not in "wise," but in "God." And it is the same with "everlasting" - it never has the force of endless in itself; and, in order to make it mean endless when applied to punishment, it must be shown that punishment is in its nature as necessarily endless and infinite as God is. It will probably take some time to do this.

It may be well to notice the argument that in Matt. xxv 46, "eternal life" and "everlasting punishment" are set against each other, and that one is as long as the other. The reply to this is, that the life of the blessed is not presumed to be endless because of the word "everlasting," but because of God's infinite goodness; the same reason which weighs against the presumption that the punishment of the wicked *is* endless. Show that there is as much reason from the nature of God to suppose that evil and suffering will be endless, as that good and happiness will be, and there may be some force to the argument.

Beside, Rom. xvi 25, 26, Titus I 2, Habak. iii. 6, show that the same word may be differently applied in the same sentence. "Everlasting hills" are not of the same continuance as the "everlasting God;" and "eternal life" is not the same as the "eternal times" (English "world"), before which it was promised. Titus I 2. [10]

The following brief summary will illustrate the scriptural usage of the words "everlasting," "forever," &c., and show how impossible it is to build up the doctrine of *endless* punishment on terms so uncertain:

"We see the word *everlasting* applied to God's covenant with the Jews; to the priesthood of Aaron; to the statutes of Moses; to the time the Jews were to possess the land of Canaan; to the mountains and hills; and to the doors of the Jewish temple. We see the word *forever* applied to the duration of a man's earthly existence; to the time a child was to abide in the temple; to the continuance of Gehazi's leprosy; to the duration of the life of David; to the duration of a king's life; to the duration of the earth; to the time the Jews were to possess the land of Canaan; to the time they were to dwell in Jerusalem; to the time a servant was to abide with his master; to the time Jerusalem was to remain a city; to the duration of the Jewish temple; to the laws and ordinances of Moses; to the time David was to be king over Israel; to the throne of Solomon; to the stones that were set up at Jordan; to the time the righteous were to inhabit the earth; and to the time Jonah was in the fish's belly. We find the phrase *forever and ever* applied to the hosts of heaven, or the sun, moon, and stars; to a writing contained in a book; to the smoke that went up from the burning land of Idumea; and to the time the Jews were to dwell in Judea. We find the word *never* applied to the time the fire was to burn on the Jewish altar; to the time the sword was to remain in the house of David; to God's covenant with the Jews; to the time the Jews should not experience shame; to the time the house of David was to reign over Israel; to the time the Jews were not to open their mouths because of their shame; to the time those who fell by death should remain in their fallen state; and to the time judgment was not executed.

But the law covenant is abolished; the priesthood of Aaron and his sons has ceased; the ordinances, and laws, and statutes of Moses are abrogated; the Jews have long since been dispossessed of the land of Canaan, have been driven from Judea, and God has brought upon them a reproach and a shame; the man to the duration of whose life the word *forever* was applied is dead; David is dead, and has ceased to reign over Israel; the throne of Solomon no longer exists; the Jewish temple is demolished, and Jerusalem has been overthrown, so that there is not left "one stone upon another;" the servants of the Jews have been freed from their masters; Gehazi is dead, and no one believes he carried his leprosy with him into the future world; the stones that were set up at Jordan have been removed, and the smoke that went up from the burning land of Idumea has ceased to ascend; the righteous do not inherit the earth endlessly, and no one believes that the mountains and hills, as such, are indestructible; the fire that burnt on the Jewish altar has long since ceased to burn; judgment has been executed; and no Christian believes that those who fall by death will never be awakened from their slumbers. Now, as these words are used in this limited sense in the Scriptures, why should it be supposed that they express endless duration when applied to punishment?" [11]

Section V. The Second Death.

The phrase "second death" is peculiar to the book of Revelations, and is found here four times only. ii 11; xx. 6, 14; xxi 8. It appears, from the context, that it is used as a figure of judgment, or punishment; and it is upon the context that we must chiefly depend, as there are no examples in the Old or New Testament, save those named, which may be appealed to as scriptural usage to determine the meaning of the expression.

It is a valuable observation of Dr. Hammond, respecting this phrase, that "it seems to be taken from the Jews, who use it proverbially for *final, utter, irrevocable destruction.*" This is unquestionably its meaning in the Revelations, being employed to point out the entire overthrow of those to whom it is applied. If the Jews were accustomed to use it proverbially in this sense, it is very likely that John, if he expected to be understood by them would use it in the same manner. And the Jews, in the habit of speaking and hearing the phrase continually with this signification, would at once understand it as descriptive of some destroying calamity or judgment. This will appear more clearly upon an examination of the several passages in which the expression "second death" is found.

"He that hath an ear, let him hear what the Spirit saith unto the churches: He that overcometh shall not be hurt of the second death." Rev. ii 11. This, it will be observed, was spoken, not to individuals, but to the church in Smyrna. In the preceding context, this church is urged, notwithstanding its trials and persecutions, to be faithful, and it should receive the crown of glory. At the close of this exhortation, the passage in review is introduced, in the way of warning, to show that the unfaithful would be hurt of the second death. Hammond says of this declaration: *"He that overcomes shall not be hurt of the second death; that is, if this church holds out constant, it shall not be cut off."* This gives the true meaning: he that overcometh, that endureth through these trials and persecutions, shall continue, and receive praise of the Lord; but he that is unfaithful, and falleth away from the truth, as an unprofitable servant, shall be hurt of the second death, shall be *cut off* and *destroyed.* And that this prediction respecting the churches of Asia was literally fulfilled, - that the candlesticks of the unfaithful were removed from their places, - history has borne ample witness; as may be seen in Keith on the Prophecies, ch. viii., and Newton's Diss. iii. After the reader shall have consulted these authors, he will see the force of Hammond's testimony, that the Jews used the expression "second death" "proverbially for final, utter, irrevocable destruction." A more perfect illustration of this use cannot be found, than in the history of those churches in relation to which the passage under consideration was spoken.

"Blessed and holy is he that hath part in the first resurrection; on such the second death hath no power, but they shall be priests of God and of Christ, and shall reign with him a thousand years." xx. 5, 6. Here, a different set of persons is introduced, and a different judgment or destruction pointed out, of course, by the "second death," though still significant of the complete downfall and ruin of those to whom it is applied. [12]

In verse 14, of this chapter, the phrase occurs again: "And death and hell were cast into the lake of fire. This is the second death." Now this looks back, without dispute, to the preceding passage, to the previous mention of the second death in connection with the first resurrection. There, the Revelator says that over those who have part in the first resurrection, the second death is to have no power, and then proceeds to describe the judgment and the condemnation, which he represents under the figure of being cast into a lake of fire, and then adds, *"This* is the second death," that is, of which I had previously spoken.

If we turn to the context, we shall find data by which to fix the time of this judgment. "I saw a great white throne, and him that sat on it, from whose face the earth and the heaven fled away; and there was no place found for them. And I saw the dead, small and great, stand before God; and the books were opened; and another book was opened, which is the book of life; and the dead were judged out of those things which were written in the books, according to their works...And whosoever was not found written in the book of life, was cast into the lake of fire." Verses 11, 12, 15.

In these verses there are several particulars which will require notice. 1. The judgment and the opening of the books. By comparing this with Dan. vii 9-14, we shall obtain some light: "And I beheld till the thrones were cast down, and the Ancient of days did sit...thousand thousands ministered unto him, and ten thousand times ten thousand stood before him: *the judgment was set, and the books were opened*...I saw in the night visions, and, behold, one like the Son of man came with the clouds of heaven, and came to the Ancient of days, and they brought him near before him. And there was given him dominion, and glory, and a kingdom, that all people, nations, and languages, should serve him: his dominion is an everlasting dominion, which shall not pass away, and his kingdom that which shall not be destroyed." From this it will be clearly seen that the judgment and the opening of the books were to take place when the kingdom should be given to the Son of man, when He should come in the clouds of heaven. He received His kingdom, and came in the clouds of heaven, when the old dispensation was abolished at the destruction of the Jewish city and temple. See Matt. xvi 27, 28; xxiv. 29-34. It is worthy of note, that this judgment from the books occurred at the *commencement of Christ's kingdom,* not at its close. 2. The Revelator represents the subjects of the judgment as dead; and Daniel (xii 2) represents them in the same manner, as "sleeping in the dust of the earth," and as coming forth at the time of judgment. 3. The Revelator says, "And whosoever was not found written in the book of life, was cast into the lake of fire," implying of course that those who were written in it were delivered. By returning again to the prophet, we find similar phraseology, which was doubtless in the mind of the Revelator: "And at that time thy people shall be delivered, every one that shall be found written in the book." xii 1.

Now, when was all this to take place? We have already seen that the deliverance was to take place at the judgment, and that this was to be when Christ received His kingdom at the abolition of the old dispensation; but happily we have direct testimony on the point, in the words immediately preceding: "At that time...there shall be a time of trouble, such as never was since there was a nation, even to that same time: *and at that time* thy people shall be delivered, every one that shall be found written in the book." xii 1. Now, by turning to Matt. xxiv. 21, we find this fact quoted by Christ, and applied to the destruction of Jerusalem: "For then shall be great tribulation, such as was not from the beginning of the world to this time." The same circumstance, and almost the same words. Here, then, we begin to see marks of the time of the judgment, the deliverance of the faithful, and the second death of the unfaithful; or, as Daniel expresses it, their "awaking to everlasting shame and contempt."

But these are not the only marks of time. When the inquiry is made in Dan. xii 6, 7, "How long shall it be to the end of these wonders?" the answer was,

"When he shall have accomplished to scatter the power of the holy people, all these things shall be finished." It is well known that the power of the holy people was scattered when their city and temple were destroyed, and they literally scattered over the face of the earth, captives and slaves among the nations. Here, then, is another mark of time.

Again, we have another mark in verse 11: "And from the time that the daily sacrifice shall be taken away, and the abomination that maketh desolate set up," &c. Now, by turning again to Matt. xxiv. 15, we find Christ quoting these very words, and applying them also to the destruction of Jerusalem: "When ye, therefore, shall see *the abomination of desolation spoken of by Daniel the prophet,* standing in the holy place (whoso readeth let him understand), then let them which be in Judea flee into the mountains," &c. More definite testimony cannot be asked.

Another mark of time is found in the passage itself, in relation to which these observations are made. In the description of the judgment which preceded the destruction represented by the figure of the "second death," the Revelator says, "I saw a great white throne, and him that sat on it, from whose face *the earth and the heaven fled away."* This language, as has often been shown, is prophetic and figurative, and is constantly used to represent the overthrow of states and kingdoms, considered both in a civil and religious aspect. For example, the destruction of Idumea is thus set forth by Isaiah: "And all the hosts of heaven shall be dissolved, and the heavens shall be rolled together as a scroll," &c. xxxiV 4, 5. And so Haggai, and Paul, who quotes him, speak of the abolition of the Jewish state and church, as a "shaking" and "removing" of the "earth" and "heaven." Hag. ii 6, 7; Heb. xii 25-29. In perfect accordance with this style, the Revelator represents the same event under the same figure: he speaks of the abolishing of the old dispensation as the fleeing away of "the earth and the heaven," and this at the time of the judgment, which, as we have seen from Daniel, was when "the abomination of desolation" was set up, and "the power of the holy people" was scattered. What renders this still more certain is, that immediately after the fleeing away of the old heaven and earth, and the infliction of the punishment of the "second death," he adds, *"And I saw a new heaven and a new earth"* (xxi 1), which language is well known to be a figure for the establishment of the Gospel kingdom; and this immediately followed the breaking up of the old dispensation, as here represented.

Lastly, the Revelator has given us one other mark of time. He says that those whom he represents as dead were judged *"every man according to their works"* (xx. 13), which we find to be the very language used by Christ in reference to the judgment at the destruction of Jerusalem: "For the Son of man shall come...and then shall he reward *every man according to his works.* Verily I say unto you, *there be some standing here which shall not taste of death till they see the Son of man coming* in his kingdom." Matt. xvi 27, 28.

Having progressed thus far, we have obtained the following results: 1. The Revelator speaks of a judgment from books, the deliverance of those written

76

in the book of life, and the destruction of the rest, described under the figure of second death. By referring to Daniel, we find him speaking of the same particulars, a judgment from books (vii 9-14), the deliverance of those written in the book (xii 1), and the destruction of others, which he represents under the figure of a resurrection to everlasting shame and contempt (xii 2). And all this he describes as taking place when the Son of man receives, or opens, His kingdom, when the abomination of desolation is set up in the holy place, the power of the holy people is scattered, and there is a time of trouble such as has never been before, - which expressions Christ quotes and applies to the destruction of the Jewish people, thereby fixing the "judgment," "deliverance," "second death," at this period. 2. In connection with these events, the judgment, &c., the Revelator represents the old heaven and earth as passing away, and a new heaven and earth as being established, - which, by comparison with the prophets, we find to be precisely the phraseology applied by them to the abolition of the Jewish dispensation at the destruction of their city and temple, and the setting up of the Gospel dispensation, thereby confining the time of judgment, &c., as being at that period. 3. The judgment described by the Revelator is according to works, which is the exact language used by Christ in reference to the judgment at the destruction of Jerusalem. These facts, taken together, lead us to the conclusion that the Revelator, Daniel, and the Savior, were all treating of one event, and that this event is the destruction of the Jewish state and church, the city and temple, to which belong the judgment, deliverance, and second death.

"But the fearful, and unbelieving, and the abominable, and murderers, and whoremongers, and sorcerers, and idolaters, and all liars, shall have their part in the lake which burneth with fire and brimstone, which is the second death." xxi 8. This passage seems to be but a repetition of what had already been said, being a specification of what was before stated in general terms. After describing the judgment, the destruction under the figure in question, and the establishment of the kingdom of Christ under the figure of the new heavens and earth, the Revelator seems, at chap. xxi 2, to have commenced a brief review or summary of what he had previously written at length, which extends through verse 8; and then apparently he begins anew at verse 9, though with yet another repetition, in the opening, in reference to the New Jerusalem, or the Gospel kingdom. In the preceding verse, he says that those who overcame, who remained faithful through trial and persecution, would inherit all things, or these things; while, in the passage in review, he reiterates, with a more particular specification of character, the destroying judgment which would fall upon the unfaithful, and upon the enemies of truth and righteousness.

It is due, perhaps, that we say a word in reference to the ground taken that the book of Revelation was written before the destruction of Jerusalem. We are not alone in this opinion; for, according to Dr. A. Clarke, it is "supported by the most respectable testimonies among the ancients," and we are sure that it is supported by the testimonies of many of the most distinguished critics of modern times, as Hentenius, Harduin, Grotius, Lightfoot, Hammond, Sir I Newton, Bp. Newton, Wetstein, &c. To these we may add Kuinoel, Lucke, Prof. Stuart, &c. The authority of such men is surely of some weight in the question. Wetstein says that the exposition of the book on the ground that it was written *before* the Jewish war, makes it "a well-connected, certain series of events," but that "the common method of interpretation, founded on the hypothesis that it was written *after* the destruction of Jerusalem, is utterly destitute of certainty." [13]

Beside this, the internal evidence is conclusive in favor of this opinion. We give a specimen: "And there was given me a reed like unto a rod, and the angel stood, saying, Rise and measure the temple of God, and the altar, and them that worship therein. But the court which is without the temple leave out, and measure it not; *for it is given unto the Gentiles;* and *the holy city* shall they tread under foot forty and two months." xi 1, 2. Here is mention of the court of the Gentiles, which could of course belong to no other temple than that at Jerusalem, as no other had such a court. Again, mention is made of the *holy city,* which was a name given exclusively to Jerusalem. And this holy city, it is said, "they *shall* tread under foot;" and, of course, it was not trodden under foot when this was written. Compare this also with Luke xxi 24: "And Jerusalem shall be trodden down of the Gentiles," &c. Once more, in chap. xi 8, we have the following: "And their dead bodies shall lie in the street of the great city, which spiritually is called Sodom and Egypt, *where also our Lord was crucified.*" This most assuredly belongs to Jerusalem, for here our Lord was crucified; and that it must have been written before its destruction, needs no proof. Enough has been offered to set forth the grounds of the position taken, that the book of Revelations was written before the destruction of Jerusalem.

This closes our inquiry with regard to the New Testament; and as yet we have found no trace of the doctrine of future endless punishment. It was the popular doctrine of the day in the time of the Savior, a part of the common faith of Jews and Pagans. Christ maintains toward it precisely the same position which Moses assumed - that of entire silence. He repudiates it by His silence on the one hand, and sets it aside on the other by teaching the doctrine of universal redemption, the great truth that in the resurrection all are equal unto the angels of God, and are children of God, being (or because) children of the resurrection. Matt. xxii; Luke xx.

It remains now to speak of the introduction of the dogma into the Christian Church, and to show the method of it. The examination will discover to us that the door for its admission was opened both from the Jewish and the Pagan side; and that the early corruption of the church encouraged its entrance, and sanctioned its continuance.

[1] Prelim. Diss. vi, Pt. ii.
[2] Lexicon on *Gehenna.* The same statements are made by Prof. Stuart, Whitby, Clarke, and others.

[3] Our Lord may refer to that great day of wrath, when the Jews and apostate Christians (He is warning against apostasy) would be destroyed amid "tribulation such as was not from the beginning of the world to that time; no, nor ever shall be." Matt. xxiV 21. It is impossible to prove *endless misery* from this passage, for the soul is involved in the same destruction with the body. The advocates of an endless life of suffering find in this text a greater stumbling-block than any other class of believers; for, if it teaches what is certain and not what is possible only, it necessitates the doctrine of annihilation.

[4] Dr. Albert Barnes says: "The extreme loathsomeness of the place, the filth and putrefaction, the corruption of the atmosphere, and the lurid fires blazing by day and by night, made it one of the most appalling and terrific objects with which a Jew was ever acquainted."

[5] Parkhurst says, "Our Lord seems to allude to the worms which continually preyed on the dead carcasses that were cast into the valley of Hinnom, Gehenna, and to the perpetual fires there kept up to consume them." *Lexicon* on the word *Gehenna.*

[6] Expositor for Sept. 1838; Schleusner's Lexicon on Asbestos; Iliad, lib. i. 599; Cruse's Eusebius, lib. vi., chap. 41. Note on page 259.

[7] Twenty of these examples repeat the word, making its actual occurrence 199 times - *eis tous aionas ton aionon.*

[8] Truth of Gospel History, p. 28.

[9] Stephens' Thesaurus Graecae Linguae; Robert Constant's Lexicon; Universalist Quarterly, ii 133, iv 5-38; Expositor, iii, &c., have furnished most of the above examples. See, also, Christian Examiner, articles by E.S. Goodwin, from Dec., 1828, to May, 1833.

[10] See Prof. Tayler Lewis on Olamic and Aeonian Words, chap. x., sect. iv.

[11] *Everlasting.* - Gen. 17:7, 8, 13; 48:4; 49:26; Exod. 40:15; Lev. 16:34; Numb. 25:13; Ps. 24:7; Hab. 3:6.

Forever. - Deut. 15:17; 1 Sam. 1:22; 27:12; Lev. 25:46; 2 Kings 5:27; Job 41:4; 1 Kings 1:31; Neh. 2:3; Dan. 2:4; Exod. 14:13; Eccl 1:4; Ps. 104:5; 78:69; Ezek. 37:25; Gen. 13:15; Exod. 32:13; Josh. 14:9; 1 Chron. 23:25; Jer. 17:25; Ps. 48:8; Jer. 31:40; 1 Kings 8:13; Numb. 10:8; 18:23; 1 Chron. 28:4; 1 Kings 9:5; Josh. 4:7; Jonah 2:6; Ps. 37:29. *Forever and ever.* - Ps. 148:5, 6; Isa. 30:8; 34:10; Jer. 7:7; 25:5. *Never.* – Lev. 6:13; 2 Sam. 12:10; Judges 2:1; Joel 2:26, 27; Jer. 33:17; Ezek. 16:63; Amos 8:14; Hab. 1:4. - *Universalist Book of Ref.,* pp. 107-177.

[12] In the preparation of this work, my rule has been, not to introduce any matter not having a direct bearing on the main question. For this reason it is sufficient to remark, that the "first resurrection" is supposed by some to signify a season of tranquillity and rest from persecution; by others, as Hammond, to represent "the flourishing condition of the Christian church, reviving after all its persecutions and corruptions;" by Mr. Whittemore, in his excellent commentary, conversion from the darkness and spiritual death of heathenism. Of course the phrase cannot be taken in a literal sense, since a *first* resurrection implies a *second;* and there can be but one literal resurrection. And the same remark applies to death, showing that the "second death" is a figure - the only question being, a figure of what? This we have endeavored to answer as above.

Chapter Six - The Introduction of the Doctrine into the Christian Church

That the first Christians brought many of their old opinions and errors with them into the Church, the New Testament itself abundantly shows. The Jewish converts clung to the Mosaic Law with strongest grasp, and sought to make it the gate through which all must enter into the Gospel kingdom.

The account given in Acts xv, and the debates in the apostolic council at Jerusalem, show how powerful were the influences from this quarter. And even Peter requires the teachings of a special vision, the sheet let down from heaven with all manner of beasts, and fowls of the air, and creeping things (Acts x.), before he can see that the law of Jewish ordinances is no longer in force, and that Jews and Gentiles must stand on the same level of faith and grace.

The epistles to the Romans and Galatians were written by Paul, the apostle of the Gentiles, expressly to combat this Jewish tendency among the first converts, and to show that salvation was not of the Law, but of grace, through faith. The impression among many of the first disciples was, that the Gospel was only a kind of expanded or perfected Judaism, that the Messiah was to establish the authority and dominion of the Law, and that all who refused to conform to the Mosaic faith and ritual, would be excluded from the privileges and blessings of His kingdom.

As we have seen, the Jews had already grossly corrupted the religion of the Law, at least the Pharisees, and the body of the people who followed them, and had adopted, among other Pagan notions, that of endless punishment. This was to be the portion of all who rejected the Law, or, in other words, of the Gentiles generally. Of course, the Jewish converts, entering the Christian church with the impression that it was only the completion of the Law, the flowering of their own religion, would take this exclusive spirit and doctrine with them, and apply them as we have seen they did in the writings already named. In Acts xv, for example, it is written: "Then rose up certain of the sect of the Pharisees, which believed (that is, converts to the Gospel), saying, that it was needful to circumcise them (the Gentiles), and to command them to keep the Law of Moses."

Speaking of the "Judaism of the infant church," Milman justly says that these "old prejudices and opinions even Christianity could not altogether extirpate or correct in the earlier Jewish proselytes, nor the perpetual tendency to contract the expanding circle, the enslavement of Christianity to the provisions of the Mosaic Law, and the spirit of the antiquated religion of Palestine."

At a later period "that exclusiveness still remained which limited the divine favor to a certain race, and would scarcely believe that foreign branches could be engrafted into the parent stock, even though incorporated with it, and still obstinately resisted the notion that Gentiles, without becoming Jews, could share in the blessings of the promised Messiah; or in their state of uncircumcision, or at least of insubordination to the Mosaic ordinances, become heirs of the kingdom of heaven."

Again he says: "A kind of latent Judaism has constantly lurked in the bosom of the Church. During the darker ages of Christianity, its sterner spirit harmonized with the more barbarous state of the Christian mind...while the great characteristic of the old religion, its exclusiveness, its restriction of the divine blessings within a narrow and visible pale, was too much in accordance both with pride and superstition, not to reassert its ancient dominion." [1]

The same statements hold good with regard to the Gentile or heathen converts. They could not in a moment divest themselves of the opinions and traditions in which they had grown up from childhood. And many of them were only half-converted, and but partially understood the doctrines and spirit of the Gospel.

St. Paul had frequent conflicts with Pagan notions both of the vulgar sort, and those that came from Oriental and Greek philosophy. His epistles abundantly show this, sometimes warning against these errors, and sometimes elaborately confuting them. "O Timothy, keep that which is committed to thy trust, avoiding profane and vain babblings, and oppositions of science, falsely so called; which some professing have erred concerning the faith." 1 Tim. vi 20, 21. "Beware lest any man spoil you through philosophy and vain deceit, after the tradition of men, after the rudiments of the world, and not after Christ." Col. ii 8. See, also, the "worshipping of angels," verse 18; and the "endless genealogies" and "fables" mentioned in 1 Tim. I 4.

Then there were some also in the church of Corinth who even denied the resurrection: "How say some among you there is no resurrection of the dead?" 1 Cor. xv Others there were who denied that Christ came in the flesh, or, in other words, that He had a real human body of flesh and blood; affirming that His body was only an appearance, and not a reality. John speaks of these in strong terms. 1 Epistle iv. 1-3; 2 Epistle 7. And in Revelations there is mention of the Nicolaitanes, a sect who mixed Pagan and Christian things together, and were half idolaters. ii 6, 15. 2 Pet. ii Beside these, there were "false teachers," who set themselves up in the church in direct opposition to the apostles, denying their authority and doctrine.

These facts show how, even while the personal disciples of Jesus were yet alive, errors and false doctrines crept into the church from the Pagan side, as well as from the Jewish. The first converts of course accepted the great historical facts of the Gospel history, but they retained also many of their old opinions, some of which were in direct opposition to the genius and doctrines of Christianity. The apostles, by their diligent watch and ready refutation, kept these Pagan tendencies measurably in check; but when they had all departed, the corruption became more rapid, and the mixture of Pagan doctrines with those of the Gospel more complete.

"Very soon after the rise of Christianity," says Enfield, "many persons, who had been educated in the schools of the philosophers, becoming converts to the Christian faith, the doctrines of the Grecian sects, and especially Platonism, were interwoven with the simple truths of pure religion.

As the Eclectic philosophy spread, Heathen and Christian doctrines were still more intimately blended, till, at last, both were almost entirely lost in the thick clouds of ignorance and barbarism which covered the earth." [2]

If the four gospels and the apostolic writings had not been preserved to us in their integrity, it would be impossible to tell what sort of a Christianity we should have had by this time. Surely it is easy enough to see how, in such a general corruption of doctrine, such a confused mixing up of Christian, Jewish and Pagan opinions and dogmas, the doctrine of endless punishments would get introduction to the church, and foothold in the creed. Both Jews and Pagans believed it; and, as we have seen, they brought with them into the church many of their old errors and heathenish superstitions and traditions, and this even in the life-time of the immediate disciples of Christ; how much more so, then, at a later period; for this amalgamation of truth and falsehood, this unseemly union of Christ and Belial, grew worse and worse from century to century.

I have not room to quote many authorities. One or two citations from Mosheim must suffice, with this prefatory remark, that one of the chief causes of the adaptation of Christian doctrines and rites to the Pagan standard was the hope of alluring them in this way into the church. "Among the Greeks and the people of the East nothing was held more sacred than their *Mysteries.* This led the Christians, in order to impart dignity to their religion, to have similar mysteries, or certain holy rites concealed from the vulgar. And they not only applied the Pagan terms, but introduced also their rites. A large part, therefore, of the Christian observances and institutions, even in this century (the second) had the aspect of the Pagan mysteries."

Speaking of the 5th century, he says, "*As no one objected to Christians retaining the opinions of their Pagan ancestors* respecting the soul, heroes, demons, temples, and the like; and as *no one proposed utterly to abolish the ancient Pagan institutions,* but only to alter them somewhat and purify them; it was unavoidable that the religion and the worship of the Christians should in this way become corrupted. This I will also add, that the doctrine of the purification of souls after death by means of some sort of fire, which afterwards became so great a source of wealth to the clergy, acquired in this age more development and a more imposing aspect."

Finally, he says, "The barriers of ancient simplicity and truth being once violated, the state of theology waxed worse and worse; and the amount of the impure and superstitious additions to the religion of Christ is almost indescribable. The controversial theologians of the East continued to darken the great doctrines of revelation by the most subtle distinctions, and I know not what philosophical jargon. Those who instructed the people at large made it their sole care to imbue them more and more with ignorance, superstition, reverence for the clergy," &c. [3]

Tytler has the following: "As the Christian religion was received, at first, by many, from the conviction of its truth from external evidence, and without a due examination of its doctrines, it was not surprising that many who called themselves Christians should retain the doctrines of a prevailing philosophy to which they had been accustomed, and endeavor to accommodate these to the system of revelation which they found in the sacred volumes. Such, for example, were the Christian Gnostics, who intermixed the doctrines of the Oriental philosophy concerning the two separate principles, a good and evil, with the precepts of Christianity, and admitted the authority of Zoroaster as an inspired personage, equally with that of Christ. Such, likewise, were the sect of the Ammonians, who vainly endeavored to reconcile together the opinions of all the schools of Pagan philosophy, and attempted, with yet greater absurdity, to accommodate all these to the doctrines of Christianity. From this confusion of the Pagan philosophy with the plain and simple doctrines of the Christian religion, the church, in this period of its infant state, suffered in a most essential manner." [4]

Other writers bear similar testimony to the manner in which Christianity was disfigured and corrupted by the introduction of Pagan dogmas and rites, and of philosophical speculations, into the place of the pure doctrines of Christ. Many of the converts to the Gospel, who had studied in the schools of heathen philosophy, entered upon the office of Christian teachers, and taking their philosophy with them, they unconsciously, in many cases, mingled it with the teachings of their new faith. "Under the bias of a strong partiality for Plato and his doctrine, many of them," says Enfield, "tinctured the minds of their disciples with the same prejudice, *and thus disseminated Platonic notions* as Christian truths; doubtless little aware how far this practice would corrupt the purity of the Christian faith, and how much confusion and dissension it would occasion in the Christian church." "A union of Platonic and Christian doctrines was certainly attempted in the second century by Justin Martyr, Athenagoras and Clemens Alexandrinus, in whose writings we frequently meet with Platonic sentiments and language, and it is not improbable that this corruption took its rise still earlier." [5]

These testimonies are sufficient to show how openly, and to what extent, the doctrines and speculations of Paganism were, at an early period, incorporated into the common faith of Christians. And surely it would be surprising if the doctrine of punishments after death, of endless punishments, which had acted so important a part in the ancient theology and politics, should not have found place among these manifold corruptions. It would be strange enough if the old fables of Hades and Tartarus were not introduced as a means of governing the ignorant multitude, and used as engines of terror against their enemies and persecutors.

And, yet, it must be confessed that we meet with very much less of this than might be expected. It is certainly a matter of wonder that we do not find the departure, on this point, from the simplicity of apostolic teaching earlier and greater than it really was. On other points the corruption of Christian doctrine began much sooner, and spread more rapidly, than on this of future endless punishment. Among the immediate successors of the apostles, either there is no allusion to it at all, or it is in a very vague and questionable manner, or coming in some other shape than that of torment.

The first Christian documents extant after the New Testament, are the writings of the apostolical fathers, or what pass under that name. It is proper to say that there is a difference of opinion among scholars as to the genuineness of a portion of these. It is generally conceded that the epistle of *Clement* of Rome is genuine; and that of *Polycarp,* with the exception of one or two interpolations. The epistle of *Barnabas* is exceedingly doubtful, and it seems certain that it could not have been the production of that Barnabas who was the companion of Paul. The *Shepherd of Hermas* was not written by the Hermas mentioned in Rom. xvi 14, but by a brother of Pius, Bishop of Rome, about the middle of the second century. The seven epistles of *Ignatius* exist in two forms, one copy very much shorter than the other, and both of them probably either forgeries outright, or largely interpolated. [6]

And, even if they were all allowed to be genuine, large allowance would be necessary in regard to the statements made in them. As Jortin remarks in regard to the Christian fathers generally, they "are often poor and insufficient guides in matters of judgment and criticism, and in the interpretation of the Scriptures, and sometimes in points of morality also, and of doctrine; as Daille, Whitby, and Barbeyrac have fully showed."

A.D. 90. CLEMENT OF ROME. The epistle of Clement contains nothing to our point. It says not a word even of future punishment, unless he refers to it in the following passage: "Shall we think it to be any very great and strange thing for the Lord of all to raise up those that religiously serve him in the assurance of a good faith?" Ch. xii, *Wake's Trans.* This might be supposed to intimate that the righteous only would be raised up by the Lord of all; but a comparison with Paul's epistle to the Romans (viii. 11), shows that this is not necessarily his meaning, as Paul certainly believed in the resurrection of all, just and unjust.

A.D. 110. IGNATIUS. Supposing the epistles ascribed to this father to be genuine, and the date given correct, we find in them nothing definite on the question in review. Speaking of those who "by wicked doctrine corrupt the faith of God," he says: "He that is thus defiled shall depart into unquenchable fire; and so also shall he that hearkens to him." Ep. iv.

Of course, nothing of endless or of future punishment can be predicated of the expression "unquenchable fire;" as our previous examination of the phrase showed its application to judgments and things of an earthly and temporal character.

The author evidently believed that the wicked would be denied a resurrection, though not annihilated, but left as disembodied spirits in Hades or the realms of the dead. He says of those who denied that Christ had a body of real flesh and blood, the same whom St. John mentions 1st Epist. iv. 2, 3, and 2d Epist. 7: "As they believe so shall it happen to them; when, being divested of the body, *they shall become mere spirits.*" Again he says: "They die in their disputes; but much better would it be for them to receive the Eucharist, that they might one day rise through it" - that is, through the body of Christ. [7]

These passages indicate that the writer thought that the wicked and unbelieving would not rise through Christ, but continue in the under-world as "mere spirits." This opinion bears mark of its Jewish origin; and it is worthy of special notice, that, so far as we know, the doctrine of future punishment makes its appearance in the Christian church in precisely the same form in which it first appeared in the Jewish church! [8] This is certainly a curious coincidence; and it is the more remarkable from the fact that at this time the doctrine of punishment after death had assumed a more positive form both among Jews and Gentiles.

A.D. 112. POLYCARP. The only thing bearing on our inquiry in the epistle of this father is the following: "Whosoever perverts the oracles of the Lord to his own lusts, and says that there shall be neither any resurrection, nor judgment, he is the first-born of Satan." [9] This passage implies the belief of Polycarp in a judgment after the resurrection; and, though nothing specific is given, it probably involved some sort of punishment to the wicked, but what sort the epistle does not hint, whether denial of a resurrection, annihilation, or positive infliction of torment.

A.D. 130-140. BARNABAS. The epistle bearing the name of this father is undoubtedly a forgery. One can hardly believe that the apostle so often mentioned in the New Testament as the friend of Paul, could write such crude and childish things as are found in this production. [10] It has a passage which says: "The way of darkness is crooked, and full of cursing; for it is the way of eternal death with punishment, in which they that walk meet with things that destroy their own souls." [11]

What the author means by "eternal death with punishment," I cannot tell; unless he believed, with Justin Martyr and others, that the wicked would be punished, and then annihilated. The phrase "destroy their own souls" may seem to confirm this supposition. He believed that Christ, after the resurrection, would judge the world, rewarding the righteous and punishing the wicked.

A.D. 150. SHEPHERD OF HERMAS. This is one of the most childish and puerile productions of the early church. It was written at Rome by a brother of Pius, then bishop of the church there. It is full of pretended visions and interviews with an angel, and the conversations on both sides, of man and angel, are as weak and insipid as the talk of those unfortunate persons called "simple."

It teaches plainly the doctrine of punishment after death, and uses the word "forever" or "eternal" in connection with it. But this, as we have seen, is not decisive of duration.

This is the sum of the evidence furnished by what are called the writings of the Apostolical Fathers. Though not all genuine, yet, if the dates have been correctly determined, they are good authority for showing the opinions of at least a portion of the Christian believers during the first half of the second century. And though we find that the doctrine of future punishment had by this time, perhaps, made its way into the church, we have no testimony to show that this punishment was believed to be endless.

On the other hand, side by side with the orthodox party, represented by these fathers, was another party known by the name of *Gnostics,* and regarded as heretics. They mixed up the speculations of Pagan philosophy with Christian doctrines, till the compound was as unintelligible as the speech of a lunatic. I refer to them only to show to what extent some of the early converts brought their old opinions and superstitions into the profession of Christianity. They differ from the orthodox party only in degree, the latter bringing less of the heathen element with them into the church. In some respects they were much nearer the simplicity of the Gospel than their opponents. [12]

It is curious, however, to note among them the doctrine of transmigration, of which we have spoken so largely in connection with the Jews. The Basilidians and Carpocratians are supposed to have believed that those who faithfully follow the Savior, ascend immediately to heaven; but that the disobedient and wicked will be punished by being sent into other bodies, of men or animals, till, purified by this transmigration, they shall be prepared to join the spirits of the blessed, and so all, at last, be saved.

And it is also worthy of notice that, though we have nothing definite from the orthodox party during this period (A.D. 90-150), respecting either endless punishment or universal restoration, they never attack the Gnostics on the score of their Universalism. They were in continual warfare with them on other points, on which they were accused of heresy; and it is fair to infer that, if this had been regarded as heresy by the orthodox party, it would have been attacked accordingly.

A.D. 140-166. JUSTIN MARTYR. This celebrated personage was a Grecian philosopher, and the first professed Christian scholar whose writings have come down to us. He was converted some thirty or forty years after the death of St. John, and entered zealously into the advocacy of the new religion, having presented two apologies, or elaborate defenses, one to the Emperor Antoninus Pius, A.D. 150; and the other to Marcus Antoninus, his successor, A.D. 162. His learning and reputation gave him a prominent place and great influence among the Christians, though he lacked judgment, was credulous, and often exceedingly absurd in his interpretation of Scripture. He suffered martyrdom at Rome about A.D. 166, and hence he is called Justin Martyr.

His conversion did not destroy his individuality, nor entirely redeem him from the bondage of the past. He retained many of his early heathen notions, and the dress and profession of a Platonic philosopher; and in some respects his creed was a sad mixture of Pagan falsehoods with Christian truths.

With regard to the subject of our inquiry, he uses the following language: "Every one is stepping forward into everlasting misery or happiness, according to his works." "Moreover we say that the souls of the wicked, being reunited to the same bodies, shall be consigned over to eternal torments, and not, as Plato will have it, to the period of a thousand years only." "Satan, with all his hosts of angels and men like himself, shall be thrust into fire, there to be tormented world without end, as our Christ hath foretold." [13]

These passages are strongly phrased, and might be taken as evidence that Justin believed in endless punishment, if there was nothing in his writings to conflict with them. The contrast between the "thousand years" of Plato and the "eternal torments" believed by the Christians of his time, would seem to indicate that "eternal" was to be taken in the sense of absolute eternity. Still it was not, evidently, so intended; for Justin did not believe in endless torments, but in the final annihilation of the wicked, as the following will show:

"Souls are not immortal," says he..."I do not say that *all* souls will die. Those of the pious will remain (after death) in a certain better place, and those of the unholy and wicked in a worse, all expecting the time of judgment. In this manner, those which are worthy to appear before God never die; but the others are tormented so long as God wills that they should exist and be tormented. Whatever does or ever will exist in dependence on the will of God, is of a perishable nature, and can be annihilated so as to exist no longer. God alone is self-existent, and by his own nature imperishable, and therefore he is God; but all other things are begotten and corruptible. For which reason souls (of the wicked) both suffer punishment and die." [14]

This shows us that Justin believed that the punishment of the wicked after death, which he describes by the terms "eternal," "world without end," &c., - and which he contrasts with the Platonic thousand years in a way significant of endless, - after all, terminated in annihilation, and was *not,* therefore, endless. Nothing, I think, can more conclusively demonstrate the uncertainty of all these forms of expression, or illustrate more forcibly the latitude of their use, and the futility of attempting to build upon them the doctrine of absolutely endless punishment. [15]

A.D. 140-150. THE SIBYLLINE BOOKS. These were pretended oracles of the famous heathen Sibyl, or prophetess, forged by some Christians about this period, for the purpose of converting the Pagans to the church. They are a miserable mixture of heathenism and Christianity, and are valuable only as evidence of the state of opinion among a portion of Christian believers at the date given.

They repeatedly declare the punishment of the wicked to be "everlasting," and yet distinctly assert that the wicked will finally be restored. After describing the horrible torments of the damned, they declare that "God will confer another favor on his worshippers, when they shall ask him; he shall save mankind from the pernicious fires and immortal agonies. This he will do. For having gathered them, safely secured from the unwearied flame, and appointed them another place," &c. [16]

The description of this "other place," which he calls the "Elysium of the immortals," shows a large admixture of Pagan elements; which was probably necessary to the purpose of the composition, viz., the conversion of Pagans. The language is adapted to their capacity and tastes; the same error which led to the monstrous corruptions alluded to in the beginning of this chapter.

A.D. 160-190. During this period we have several productions which employ the usual phrases in regard to the subject, such as "everlasting fire," "eternal punishment," and their equivalents. The last date brings us to the distinguished IRENAEUS, bishop of Lyons, in France. He taught that the wicked would be cast into *inextinguishable and eternal fire.* And yet he did not believe that they would be punished endlessly, for he undoubtedly adopted the doctrine of the final annihilation of the disobedient and unrighteous. He says: "The principle of existence is not inherent in our own constitutions, but is given us of God; and the soul can exist only so long as God wills. He who cherishes the gift of existence, and is thankful to the Giver, shall exist forever; but he who despises it, and is ungrateful, deprives himself of the privilege of existing forever."..."He who is unthankful to God for this temporal life, which is little, cannot justly expect from him an existence which is endless." [17]

These extracts from his work against heretics, are clear proof that he was of the same opinion with Justin Martyr, that the souls of the wicked will be annihilated after a period of punishment in "everlasting fire." For he believed they would be sent into this fire after the judgment, which was to succeed the resurrection, according to his creed. His words are: "Evil spirits, and the angels who sinned and became apostates, and the impious, and the unjust, and the breakers of the law, and the blasphemers among men, he will send into everlasting fire."

A.D. 200-220. TERTULLIAN. This father was originally a Pagan; by birth, an African, and a lawyer by profession. He seems to have believed in the strictly endless punishment of the wicked, and to have argued against the doctrine of their annihilation, or, to use his own words, against the doctrine that "the wicked would be consumed, and not punished," that is, endlessly.

He is the first, as far as can be ascertained, who expressly affirmed, and argued the question, that the torments of the damned would be equal in duration to the happiness of the blessed.

Tertullian was of a fierce and fiery temper, when provoked, and seems a fitting personage to stand godfather in the infernal baptism by which this doctrine was received into the Christian church. He discourses on the subject of hell-torments in the following exultant strain:

"You are fond of your spectacles," said he to the Pagans; "but there are other spectacles; that day disbelieved, derided by the nations, the last and eternal day of judgment, when all ages shall be swallowed up in one conflagration; what a variety of spectacles shall then appear! How shall I admire, how laugh, how rejoice, how exult, when I behold so many kings, and false gods in heaven, together with Jove himself, groaning in the lowest abyss of darkness! - so many magistrates, who persecuted the name of the Lord, liquefying in fiercer flames than they ever kindled against Christians; so many sage philosophers blushing in raging fire, with their scholars whom they persuaded to despise God, and to disbelieve the resurrection; and so many poets shuddering before the tribunal, not of Rhadamanthus, not of Minos, but of the disbelieved Christ! Then shall we hear the tragedians more tuneful in the expression of their own sufferings; then shall we see the dancers far more sprightly amidst the flames; the charioteer all red-hot in his burning car; and the wrestlers hurled, not upon the accustomed list, but upon a plain of fire." [18]

The man who could write this may well be allowed the honor of giving to the monstrous doctrine of endless torments a place in the Christian church; and we should have selected him, of all others, as its fitting representative in spirit, and in the savage and vindictive character of his feelings towards his enemies.

And now that we have the foul thing fairly introduced among the professed followers of the Gospel, let us note the steps of its progress, and mark its growth from the first departure from the simplicity of Christ, to the full development of the monster in the time of Tertullian.

First. The denial of a resurrection to the wicked and unbelieving, the soul remaining in Hades as a disembodied spirit. A.D. 110, or some ten years after the death of St. John.

Second. The judgment after death, and the punishment of the unbelieving and wicked. A.D. 112-140.

Third. The future torment, and final annihilation, of the souls of the wicked. A.D. 140-190.

Fourth. The future endless torment of the wicked, as set forth by Tertullian. A.D. 200-220. [19]

These seem to be the steps forward, the method of growth, which marked the reception of the old Pagan doctrine into the faith of the Christians. And the great wonder is that, considering the extent to which this dogma was received among both Jews and heathens, it did not get foothold in the church before; especially when we remember how rapidly other philosophical speculations and Pagan notions prevailed to the corruption of the pure doctrines of Christ. And yet it takes a hundred and seventy years from the death of Christ, and a hundred from the last of His personal disciples, to establish this abomination as a part of the Christian creed.

Nay, this is granting more than the facts will warrant, for it cannot be said to have been established as an article of belief at this period, but only that it was received by some Christians. Others did not receive it at all; and the Gospel doctrine of universal restoration was held by some of the most eminent of the Christian fathers at the same time Tertullian and others avowed their faith in endless punishment.

But slowly the corruption spread, and little by little the Pagan dogma gained upon the Christian doctrine, till at last, partly in consequence of personal quarrels among those concerned, the primitive teaching on this point was condemned in a Church council held A.D. 553 (or 540); and the doctrine of endless punishment sanctioned as a fundamental article of Christian faith. I repeat again, it is truly wonderful, considering the general corruption of the church in these centuries, *that it should take five hundred years for this favorite Pagan dogma to get itself established as orthodoxy!* Yet such is the fact. [20]

In order to prevent all misunderstanding on the point in question, and for the purpose of shutting off any misrepresentation of the real position here assumed, I must call attention again to the fact, already mentioned in chapter v, section iv, and partly illustrated in this chapter, that the early writers of the church frequently speak of "everlasting" or "eternal punishment." But these expressions are used just as freely by those who are known to believe in the annihilation of the wicked, and by those who are acknowledged on all hands as believers in universal redemption; so that these phrases are no evidence of a belief in *endless* punishment. There is a great difference, as the Scriptures show, between "eternal" or "everlasting," and "endless."

For example: Justin Martyr and Irenaeus say the wicked will be condemned to *everlasting* punishment, and *after* this will be annihilated. So the author of the Sibylline Oracles, Clement of Alexandria, Origen, Titus, Bishop of Bostra, Gregory, &c., use the phrase "everlasting" or "eternal punishment" without reserve, though they were acknowledged Universalists. It is plain, therefore, that *aionios* or "eternal" was not employed by them in the sense of *endless;* and that the use of this phraseology among the early Christians is no evidence of their belief in endless torments.

Augustine, who flourished about A.D. 400 to 430, was the first to argue that *aionios* signified strictly *endless.* He attempted a criticism on the original word, maintaining at first that it always meant endless; but this being so bold and palpable a blunder, he was compelled to abandon it, admitting that it did not *always* mean endless, but did *sometimes;* and he brings Matt. xxv 46, as proof, arguing that if the "everlasting punishment" was not endless, the "eternal life" was not. And this criticism has been handed down from his time to the present, and is still employed with great confidence, notwithstanding it forces into the spiritual world a judgment which the Savior expressly declared should take place in that generation, before some then living should die. Matt. xxiv. 30-34; xvi 28; Luke ix. 26, 27.

I have now followed the inquiry respecting the origin of the doctrine of Endless Punishment and its introduction among the Jews and Christians, as far as the purpose I have in view seems to require. The object has been to furnish the reader with an outline, simply, of the argument, to present the method of inquiry, and facts and authorities enough to justify the conclusions. It is possible that the facts and citations may be new to many believers in this doctrine, not accustomed to examine the foundations of their belief; and it may induce some to enter into an inquiry on the general subject, more thorough and critical than the narrow limits assigned to this sketch would allow.

Only one thing remains to complete the plan originally proposed to myself, and that is to illustrate briefly, from history and facts, the influence of the doctrine on society, and on the morals and happiness of its believers. It is a just rule established by the Savior, that "the tree is known by its fruits;" and though great caution should be used in any attempt to connect conduct directly with faith, as an evidence of its moral tendencies, yet I think in this case the connection and dependence are so obvious, there is little danger of any serious error. The history of the doctrine of Endless Punishment, in its effects on the character and action of those believing it, is one of the most painful and shocking in the annals of mankind; and I know of nothing which exposes with a more terrible eloquence the shallowness of the remark so often made, that "it is no matter what a man believes, if he only lives right." *If he lives right!* - but, in order to live right, he must believe right, or at least he must not believe wrong. Always, as history witnesses, the disposition, character and practices of the individual, or of a people, have been formed, or in all important features modified, by the character and spirit of their religion or of the deity or deities worshipped by them.

This I shall illustrate in respect to the doctrine in review; and, shall endeavor to show that, with the Christian as well as with other men, a savage creed, if left unchecked to do its legitimate work, will beget a savage temper and a corresponding conduct; or, in one word, that "a corrupt tree cannot bring forth good fruit."

[1] Milman's Hist. of Christianity, Book ii, chap. ii See also the same in substance in Neander, vol. I, p. 3, 4, &c; Mosheim vol. I, cent. 1; and Conybeare's Life and Epistles of St. Paul, vol. I, pp. 441-459. Chrysostom complains that the Christians of the 4th century, even, are half Jews. Between the two corrupting forces, Jewish and Pagan, the pure doctrines of the Gospel had little chance of coming out of the conflict unharmed; and the facts show that they did not.
[2] History of Philosophy, *Preliminary Obs.* See also Book vi, ch. ii, where he repeatedly states "the fathers of the church departed from the simplicity of the apostolic age, and corrupted the purity of the Christian faith," "disseminated Platonic notions as Christian truths," &c.
[3] Murdock's Mosheim, cent. ii, iv., V, vi *History of Theology.* See also Neander's History of Christianity, vol. I 248-254.

[4] Tytler's Universal History, Book V, chapter iv.

[5] For additional testimony see chap. x., sect. v.

[6] I have used these writings of the so-called apostolic fathers, in argument, elsewhere; but a more careful inquiry into their authority has shaken my faith in their genuineness, or their purity, to the extent named above.

[7] Epistle to the Smyrneans, chapts. 1. 8, ii 17. Wake's Translation. Compare with Epistle to Trallians and Romans.

[8] See chapter iv.

[9] Epistle to Philippians, ii Compare this passage with what Paul says of the same class, 1 Cor. xv 12, and 2 Tim. ii 18.

[10] See Norton's Genuineness of the Gospels, Note F., on the Apostolical Fathers.

[11] Epistle, chapters xv, iv.

[12] If I were to institute a comparison between the two parties at this period, it would be something like this: That the faith of the Orthodox party was one half Christian, one quarter Jewish, and one quarter Pagan; while that of the Gnostic party was about one quarter Christian and three quarters philosophical Paganism. It is to be remembered, however, that all we know of the Gnostics comes to us through the writings of their enemies, and that, therefore, large allowances are to be made for misrepresentation.

[13] First Apology, translated by W. Reeves, London, 1709, pp. 26, 31, 59. I do not know how far the translation is reliable, and have no means at hand of comparing with the original the expressions "world without end," "everlasting misery," &c., but suppose the Greek in these cases to be *aion* and its derivations.

[14] Dialogue with Trypho, cited in the Ancient History of Universalism, p. 58, 1st edit.

[15] Justin acknowledges that the doctrine of a future "just retribution of rewards and punishments was a current opinion in the world," and that God was "pleased to *second this notion* by the prophetic spirit." This is a curious confession; that God was not the original mover, but only seconded the motion! With singular inconsistency he says, in another place, that "the philosophers and poets took their hints of punishment after death, &c., from the prophets." We have already shown that they make not the slightest allusion to any such thing. *First Apology*, p. 79.

[16] Ancient History of Universalism, p. 52; Murdock's Mosheim, I 130; and especially Milman's History of Christianity, B. ii chap. 7.

[17] Ancient Hist. of Universalism, chap. ii, sec. xi, where the references are given to the work against the heretics.

[18] Guizot attempts to soften the translation of Gibbon, but Milman frankly owns that "it would be wiser for Christianity, retreating upon its genuine records in the New Testament, to disclaim this fierce African, than to identify itself with his furious invectives, by unsatisfactory apologies for their unchristian fanaticism." Decline and Fall, chap. xv, Note 72 and the text.

Jortin says: "Tertullian had no small share of credulity; he proves the soul is *corporeal* from the visions of an *illuminated sister,* who told him she had seen a soul! (Probably a *'medium.'* Here is a touch of the delusion of our day, in which Tertullian seems to have been a believer.) He affirms roundly that a fine city was seen for forty days suspended in the air over Jerusalem." Remarks on Ecc. Hist., vol. ii 81. Whether such a man's belief of endless punishment is of any importance, as regards the question of its truth or divine origin, the reader can judge.

[19] It will be observed that just in the ratio the church departs, in time, from Christ, and becomes corrupt and heathenish, just in that ratio the punishment of the wicked increases in cruelty. Compare the *first* doctrine and date, A.D. 110, with the *fourth,* A.D. 220, when the abomination is complete.

[20] It may edify the reader, and enable him to put a just value on the wisdom of this council, to know that the same decree which established the orthodoxy of endless punishment, also established, as a fundamental article of Christian faith, that "mankind, in the resurrection, *will rise in an erect posture!"*

Chapter Seven - The Doctrine Creates A Cruel and Revengeful Spirit - Illustrated from History

It matters not by what name a man is called, whether Pagan, Jew, or Christian; nor matters it at all where the lot of life has fallen to him, whether in a land over which broods the night of heathenism, or on which rests the radiant light of the Gospel. He is still a man, though a Christian; he is born, lives, and dies; he thinks and feels, hopes and fears, rejoices and sorrows, after the manner of all other men. Hence, if the Christian believe in a cruel religion, believe in it with all his heart, it will make him cruel; it will certainly harden his heart. If he believe in and worship a God of a merciless and ferocious character, this will eventually be, visibly or invisibly, his own character. If he believe the God of the Bible hates any portion of mankind, or regards them with any dislike or displeasure, he also will come to hate them, and to entertain towards them the same feelings which he supposes reside in the bosom of God. If he believe that God will, in expression of those feelings, or for any reason, devote them to flame and torture hereafter, it is natural and necessary that he should infer it would be, for the same reason, acceptable to God that he should devote them to flame and torture here. And if the degree of civilization and the condition of society shall permit; or, in other words, if no power from without prevent, he will assuredly do this, as a most acceptable offering to Heaven; and to the utmost of his power will conform to what he believes to be the disposition and wishes of God in this respect.

And this is not said without ample means for proving the correctness of the statement. The history of Christianity, so called, in all ages and among every people, and in every form which it has taken, will abundantly establish the truth of the position, that the temper and practice of a people is determined by the spirit of their religion and their gods.

It is not necessary to enter into a labored description of the doctrines of the Christian church in the days of its darkness and corruption, nor of the awful and revolting views entertained of God, of His disposition towards man, of His government, laws and punishments. It is enough that Paganism in its worst forms has never surpassed, if it has equaled, the savage and terrible descriptions which have been given by Christians of their God. The character ascribed to Him; the dreadful wrath and vengeance with which He is moved; the cold and malignant purpose of creation in regard to millions of souls; the stern severity and gloom of His government; the horrible and never-ceasing tortures which He will inflict on His helpless children - all this, and much more of like character, defies the power of language to set it forth in its true light, or to present it in a manner adequate to its shocking and revolting reality. I give a single example:

Dr. Benson, an eminent English minister, in a sermon on "The Future Misery of the Wicked," says, "God is present in hell, in his infinite justice and almighty wrath, as an unfathomable sea of liquid fire, where the wicked must drink in everlasting torture. The presence of God in his vengeance scatters darkness and woe through the dreary regions of misery. As heaven would be no heaven if God did not there manifest his love, so hell would be no hell if God did not there display his wrath. It is the presence and agency of God which gives everything virtue and efficacy, without which there can be no life, no sensibility, no power." He then adds, "God is, therefore, himself present in hell, to see the punishment of these rebels against his government, that it may be adequate to the infinity of their guilt: his fiery indignation kindles, and his incensed fury feeds the flame of their torment, while his powerful presence and operation maintain their being, and render all their powers most acutely sensible; thus setting the keenest edge upon their pain, and making it cut most intolerably deep. He will exert all his divine attributes to make them as wretched as the capacity of their nature will admit."

After this he goes on to describe the duration of this work of God, and calls to his aid all the stars, sand, and drops of water, and makes each one tell a million of ages; and when all those ages have rolled away, he goes over the same number again, and again, and so on forever.

Yet, Christians have believed all this; have believed that God is the enemy of the sinner and unbeliever; that He regards with a fierce displeasure those of a wrong faith or a wrong life; that heretics and the impenitent are an abomination in His sight; and that upon these wretched victims the vials of His wrath will finally be broken, and overwhelm them in endless and irretrievable ruin. As remarked, it will not need that we should give a lengthened or labored review of this point. A more important question is that which regards the influence of this savage creed upon the believer. To this let us give some attention, and we shall find, what we may expect, that its tendency in all ages, when believed in right earnest, has been to harden the heart, to brutalize the affections, and render those receiving it, under any of its forms, cruel, and ferocious in disposition, and, so far as circumstances would allow, in practice.

Take as a worthy example the celebrated passage of Tertullian, already quoted: "How shall I admire, how laugh, how rejoice, how exult, when I behold so many kings and false gods, together with Jove himself, groaning in the lowest abyss of darkness! so many magistrates who persecuted the name of the Lord, liquefying in fiercer flames than they ever kindled against Christians; so many sage philosophers, with their deluded scholars, blushing in raging fire!" &c.

Without doubt, Tertullian was of a fierce and bitter spirit, independently of his religious faith; but this fiery ebullition of hate and ferocity serves to show how perfectly fitted that faith was to add fuel to the flame, and what an ample field and congenial scenes it furnished for his savage nature to revel in. Under the influence of such a belief, his wild temper gathered new vigor, his revengeful feelings were cultivated and strengthened to a frightful degree, till at last he comes to rejoice and exult in the agonies of the damned with a relish that a devil might envy. One cannot but see that it only needed the power to have engaged this ferocious man in the work of torture on earth, the prospect of which in hell he contemplated with such fiendish delight.

A further illustration may be found in the crusades against the Albigenses in the thirteenth century, one of the darkest and bloodiest pages in the history of any religion, Christian or Pagan. The sacrifices of the Goth and Mexican, and the revolting cruelties of the Polynesian and the negro of Dahomy, are scarcely equal to the savage butcheries and the shocking barbarities inflicted by the Catholic crusader, in the name of his God, upon this gentle and virtuous people. No passage in the history of man is more to the purpose of our argument, or more conclusive of the direct influence of religious faith upon the temper and character, than that in which are recorded the persecutions and sufferings of these unhappy reformers. Throughout the whole of this merciless crusade, and amid all its scenes of burning and desolation, of murder and torture, the cry of the ruthless priest was heard, "It is for the glory of God!" And the brutal multitude, believing that they were doing God a service, and securing their own salvation by the slaughter of heretics, rushed forward to the bloody work with the ferocity of tigers and the joy of a Tertullian.

Sismondi says, speaking of the deliberate savageness of the monks who occupied the pulpits, and urged on the people to this diabolical work, they "showed how every vice might be expiated by crime; how remorse might be expelled by the flames of their piles; how the soul, polluted with every shameful passion, might become pure and spotless by bathing in the blood of heretics. By continuing to preach the crusade, they impelled, each year, waves of new fanatics upon those miserable provinces; and they compelled their chiefs to recommence the war, in order to profit by the fervor of those who still demanded human victims, and required blood to effect their salvation." They represented this inoffensive people as the outcasts of the human race, and the especial objects of divine hatred and vengeance; and no devotional exercise, no prayer or praise, no act of charity or mercy, was half so acceptable to God as the murder of a heretic.

"The more zealous, therefore, the multitude were for the glory of God, the more ardently they labored for the destruction of heretics, the better Christians they thought themselves. And if at any time they felt a movement of pity or terror, whilst assisting at their punishment, they thought it a revolt of the flesh, which they confessed at the tribunal of penitence; nor could they get quit of their remorse till their priests had given them absolution." "Amongst them all not a heart could be found accessible to pity. Equally inspired by fanaticism and the love of war, they believed that the sure way to salvation was through the field of carnage. Seven bishops, who followed the army, had blessed their standards and their arms, and would be engaged in prayer for them while they were attacking the heretics. Thus did they advance, indifferent whether to victory or martyrdom, certain that either would issue in the reward which God himself had destined for them." [1]

And most frightfully did they do the work of religious butchery and cruelty. Like the Scandinavian pirates, wherever they went they desolated with fire and sword, sparing neither age, nor sex, nor condition. They even wreaked their furious vengeance on inanimate objects, destroying houses, trees, vines, and every useful thing they could reach, leaving all behind a wide and blackened waste, marked by smoldering and smoking ruins, and the dead and putrefying bodies of murdered men, women, and children.

At the taking of Beziers the wretched sufferers fled to the churches for protection, but their savage enemies slaughtered them on the very altars, and filled the sanctuaries with their mangled bodies. And when the last living creature within the walls had been slain, and the houses plundered, the crusaders set fire to the city in all directions at once, and so made of it one huge funeral pile. Not a soul was left alive, nor a house left standing! During the slaughter one of the knights inquired of a fierce priest how they should distinguish between Catholics and heretics.

"Kill them all!" was his reply, *"the Lord will know his own."* In this one affair from twenty to thirty thousand human beings perished, because the religion of their butchers assured them that such bloody sacrifices would be acceptable to God.

But the priests and crusaders were not content with simple murder. It was often preceded by the most exquisite cruelties. De Montfort on one occasion seized a hundred prisoners, cut off their noses, tore out their eyes, and sent them with a one-eyed man as a guide to the neighboring castles to announce to the inhabitants what they might expect when taken. And often, as matter of amusement, so hardened had they become, they subjected their victims to the most dreadful tortures, and rejoiced in their wild cries of agony, and manifested the highest delight at the writhings and contortions of the dying wretches. So perfectly fiendish had these fanatics grown through the influence of their religious belief! And what can more clearly show the connection between faith and practice, or more conclusively demonstrate the truth that the worshipper will be like his god, than the revolting barbarities inflicted upon these humble and innocent people, on the ground that they were hated

96

of the Deity, and devoted by Him to the flames and torments of an endless hell! Verily, the Christian is but a man, and that which makes the Pagan ferocious and blood-thirsty will produce the same effect upon him.

The massacre of St. Bartholomew is another terrible proof of the power of religious faith to convert man into a fiend. As a single exhibition of slaughter and cruelty in the name of God and religion, this is perhaps the most monstrous, and on a more fearful scale, than any before or since. Probably thirty or forty thousand victims perished in Paris and in the provinces in this one butchery! And it would be almost impossible to describe the variety of forms in murder, or to give a catalogue of the cruelties practiced. Even children of ten or twelve years engaged in the work of blood, and were seen cutting the throats of heretic infants!

But what is the most impious of all is the manner in which the news of this massacre was received at Rome by the Church and its head. The courier was welcomed with lively transports, and received a large reward for his joyful news. The pope and his cardinals marched in solemn procession to the church of St. Mark to acknowledge the special providence; high mass was celebrated; and a jubilee was published, that the whole Christian world might return thanks to God (!) for this destruction of the enemies of the church in France. In the evening, the cannon of castle St. Angelo were fired, and the whole city illuminated with bonfires, in expression of the general joy for this dreadful slaughter. [2]

And when we remember that all this was done in the name of Christianity and the church, that it was deemed a grateful offering to God, who, it is supposed, hates heretics, and will give them over to torments infinitely greater than these, and endless, we shudder to think how terrible an engine is superstition, and how nearly it has turned the Christian church into a slaughter-house! Truly, one has well said: "The ancient Roman theater, with its mere sprinkling of blood, and its momentary pangs and shrieks, quite fades if brought into comparison with that Coliseum of Papal cruelty, in which not a hundred or two of victims, but myriads of people - yes, nations entire - have been gorged!" [3]

To complete the picture of depravity and cruelty, and confirm the argument for the influence of religion on the heart and life, we need only refer to that thrice-accursed institution, the INQUISITION! In this was concentrated all that was monstrous and revolting. It were impossible to put into words sufficiently expressive the abominable principles upon which its ministers proceeded in their persecutions, or the cold, deliberate, malignant ferocity with which they tortured their miserable victims. Every species of torment was invented that the united talents of the inquisitors could devise; and the protracting of life under the most excruciating agonies, so that the poor wretch might endure to the last degree, was reduced to a perfect system. The annals of Pagan sacrifice, with all its horrors, furnish no parallel to the atrocities of the Romish Inquisition. [4] The blackest and bloodiest page in the history of superstition is that which bears the record of inquisitorial bigotry and ferocity. One would think that even hell itself might applaud the refinement of cruelty, were not the devils kept silent through envy of the superior skill and savageness of their earthly rivals.

But this terrible influence was not confined to the priests of this religion; the cruel and ferocious spirit of it was diffused abroad among all its believers; and its pestilential breath spread over the whole social life of the people. Informers were encouraged, heretics were hunted, private hatred took its revenge, and the most malignant passions of the corrupt heart were roused into action in the service of God and the church. Even the tenderest ties of affection, and the holiest relations of life, were crushed beneath the iron heel of religious zeal. Husbands betrayed their wives, and parents their children, and sisters their brothers, and gave them up to the cruelties of the holy office, and to the flames of the auto-da-fe; and, so doing, congratulated themselves upon their fidelity to God, measured by their triumph over the loveliest attributes of humanity. [5] So mighty, in this case also, was the power of a savage religion to crush every kindly feeling, every emotion of love and pity, and to train its followers to cruelty and blood.

But this influence is not confined to Catholics; it is found wherever the doctrines of which it is the offspring are found. The history of Calvin and Servetus shows the same savage faith, having the power, doing the same infernal work. And the history of the Puritans of our own land, of the Dissenters of England, of the Covenanters of Scotland, of the Jews everywhere, discovers also the same faith; shorn of its power, to be sure, by the progress of society and civil institutions, but, with a change of circumstances, ready at any time to seize the dagger or the torch, and spring forth to the work of death. Reluctant as we may be to admit it, we cannot blind ourselves to these facts. The cruel butcheries of the past, the dungeon, the rack, the fagot, the bloody scourge falling upon the back of the meekly suffering Quaker, the cry of agony, the unheeded prayer for mercy - all these in the past; - and the exceeding bitterness, the fierce clamor and unblushing falsehoods of controversy in the present; the refusal of the common courtesies of life, or the stern hate that often lurks beneath outward civility; the malignant sneer at the labors of those who seek to unfold the truth of God's saving love for all; the half exultation at any seeming proof of the final triumph of evil and the ceaseless torments of the wicked; the hardness of heart with which this result is sometimes contemplated, and the indifference with which one sect devotes another to this awful doom - all these show clearly that the Christian is subject to the same law which governs other men; show with a painful distinctness that, so far as the refining influences of literature and civilization would permit, the belief in a ferocious god and an endless hell have done their legitimate work upon his heart. Like the Aztec of America, and the Norseman of Europe, he has partaken of the spirit of his deity, and, supposing it a duty and a most acceptable service, he begins, so far as he can in this world, the work of torment which he believes his unforgiving god will make infinite and endless in the next.

Queen Mary of England was right when, as Bp. Burnet says, she defended her bloody persecutions by appealing to the supposed example of the Deity: "As the souls of heretics are hereafter to be eternally burning in hell, there can be nothing more proper than for me to imitate the divine vengeance by burning them on earth." This is legitimate and logical reasoning, and exhibits the natural fruits of the doctrine.

If, then, we would make mankind what they should be, we must begin with the object of their worship; we must first make their religion what it should be. We must cast out from the holy place all the dark and ferocious superstitions of the past and the present, whether Pagan or Christian, and in the place of these set up, in all its divine beauty and simplicity, the merciful and loving religion of Jesus Christ. The views which this unfolds of God the Father, of His government and its final issues, can alone be favorable to the spiritual progress of humanity, can alone form the heart of man to gentleness and goodness, and recreate it in the image of heaven. "National religions," says a celebrated German, "will not become the friends of virtue and happiness until they teach that the Deity is not only an inconceivably powerful, but also an inconceivably wise and good being; that for this reason He gives way neither to anger nor revenge, and never punishes capriciously; that we owe to His favor alone all the good that we possess and enjoy; that even our sufferings contribute to our highest good, and death is a bitter but salutary change; in fine, that the sacrifice most acceptable to God consists in a mind that seeks for truth, and a pure heart. Religions which announce these exalted truths offer to man the strongest preservatives from vice, and the strongest motives to virtue, exalt and ennoble his joys, console and guide him in all kinds of misfortunes, and inspire him with forbearance, patience, and active benevolence towards his brethren." [6] Even so; let this be the religion of the nations, and soon the world shall be getting forward toward heaven. And it was to reveal these truths, and to bring them near to the heart of humanity, that Jesus gave His life, and labored with all the earnestness of His loving heart.

Let this, then, be the religion of the Christian, and he will be a Christian indeed. Let him believe in God as the parent of all, as the dispenser of life and good to all; let him see Him as Christ saw Him, clothed in robes of light and mercy, and he will love as Christ loved, and, so far as he may, will live as Christ lived. Let him believe that God always blesses, and he will not dare, he will not wish, to curse whom God hath blessed. Let him believe that God never hates, is never angry; and, that he may be like Him, and approved of Him, he will diligently seek to expel all hatred and passion from his own heart. Let him believe that all men are brethren, journeying homeward to the presence of the Father, where, delivered from all evil, we shall be as the angels; and that it is the earnest entreaty of this Father that we should not fall out by the way, but bear each other's burdens, and love one another as He loves us, loves the world: let these be the Christian's views of God, and he shall indeed be born again from above. Let this be the religion of the nations, and

"Earth shall be paradise again,
And man, O God, thine image here."

[1] Sismondi's History of Crusades against the Albigenses, chap. ii 73-84, &c. The reader will doubtless be reminded of a passage from Wheaton's Northmen. "The religion of Odin stimulated the thirst of blood by promising the joys of Valhalla (heaven) as the reward of those who fell gloriously in battle." Which is the better, the religion of the Northman or the Catholic? The former has at least the redeeming feature of bravery, while the last is distinguished only for its ferocity. Mahomet might be justly indignant if compared with Simon de Montfort.

[2] See the fiendish letter of the pope to the French king on this occasion, in Smedley's History of the Reformed Religion in France, chap. ix.

[3] Natural History of Fanaticism, sect. vi I would recommend this work to the perusal and study of every clergyman, and every individual, in the land. It is the production of an original thinker, and an eloquent writer. The comparison of the Roman soldier and the *Christian* monk, in the sixth section, is seldom surpassed simply as a piece of composition, aside from its graphic truth and power.

[4] Prescott, speaking of the Aztec or Mexican human sacrifices and the Inquisition, gives the preference to the former; for the Inquisition, he remarks, not only "branded its victims with infamy in this world, but consigned them to everlasting perdition in the next." Vol. I, p. 84. So on page 77 he says: "Few will sympathize, probably, with the sentence of Torquemada, who concludes his tale of woe by coolly dismissing the soul of the victim (of Mexican sacrifice) to sleep with those of his false gods in hell."

[5] In Spain the Inquisition has the strongest hold. Its effects are thus described by M'Crie: "Possessing naturally some of the finest qualities by which a people can be distinguished - generous, feeling, devoted, constant - the Spaniards became cruel, proud, reserved and jealous. The revolting spectacles of the auto-da-fe, continued for so long a period, could not fail to have the most hardening influence on their feelings. In Spain, as in Italy, religion is associated with crime, and protected (protects it?) by its sanctions. Thieves and prostitutes have their images of the Virgin, their prayers, their holy water, and their confessions. Murderers find a sanctuary in the churches and convents. Crimes of the blackest character are left unpunished in consequence of the immunities granted to the clergy." - History of the Reformation in Spain, chap. ix. See also Smedley's, D'Aubigne's, and Burnett's Histories. For this last may be substituted, as more brief and popular in its form, a work published by the London Religious Tract Society, republished by the Harpers, entitled "The Days of Queen Mary." For a short but interesting notice of the Inquisition in Goa, see Buchanan's Christian researches, pp. 172-193.

[6] Biblical Repository for April, 1843. Dr. Robertson also has a striking passage on this point, and confirmatory of the general argument, which, notwithstanding its length, I cannot refuse to quote. Speaking of the Peruvians, he says: "The sun, as the great source of light, of joy and felicity, in the creation, attracted their principal homage...By directing their veneration to that glorious luminary, which, by its universal and vivifying energy, is the best emblem of divine beneficence, the rites which they deemed acceptable to him were innocent and humane. They

offered to the sun a part of those productions which his genial warmth had called forth from the bosom of the earth, and reared to maturity. They sacrificed, as an oblation of gratitude, some of the animals which were indebted to his influence for nourishment. They presented to him choice specimens of those works of ingenuity which his light had guided the hand of man in forming. But the Incas never stained their altars with human blood, nor could they conceive that their beneficent father, the sun, would be delighted with such horrid victims. Thus the Peruvians, unacquainted with those barbarous rites which extinguish sensibility, and suppress the feelings of nature at the sight of human sufferings, were formed by the spirit of the superstition which they had adopted, to a national character more gentle than that of any people in America." History of America, B. vii sect. 36. See also the note to this section, 42.

Chapter Eight - The Comparative Moral Influence of Belief and Disbelief in Endless Punishment - Historical Contrast

In this chapter I propose, by historical contrast, to show the influence of endless punishment, and of its opposite, on the general morals of society.

It is believed by most Christian sects that this doctrine is the great regulator of social and individual morality. Nothing has been more frequently and urgently pressed upon public attention, than the necessity of future endless punishments as the reward of impenitent sinners. It is argued that it is the only restraint which is effectual in checking presumptuous transgressors, and that the fear of this removed from the minds of men, and the world would speedily become a perfect social wreck, the very likeness of the infernal pit itself. With all possible sincerity this view of the question has been urged by many honest-minded Christians, from the pulpit and from the press, in full belief that the danger is real.

And yet in the very face of this argument, stands the whole heathen world, believing this doctrine for ages prior to the coming of Christ, and yet, at the time of His coming, utterly lost in corruption and depravity, in daily practice of the most abominable vices and crimes, and the whole mass of society sunk in the lowest depths of infamy, shame and wickedness. What sort of restraining influence did the doctrine of endless punishment have on them?

The Jews, also, as we have seen, were believers in this doctrine in the time of Christ; and their corruption and wickedness at that period, and later, are almost proverbial. Josephus witnesses to this in the most positive language. "I cannot say it without regret," are his words, "but I must declare it as my opinion, that if the Romans had delayed to come against these wretches, the city (Jerusalem) would have been swallowed up by an earthquake, or overwhelmed by a deluge, or else been consumed by fire from heaven, as Sodom was; for it produced a generation of men more wicked than those who had suffered such calamities." Again he says: "To reckon up all their villainies is impossible; but never did any city suffer so great calamities; nor was there ever, from the beginning of the world, a time more fruitful of wickedness than that was." [1]

So little influence did the doctrine have on the Jews in the way of restraint. Such testimonies of the moral condition of those believing it, do not go far toward fortifying the large claims set up for its conservative and sanctifying power. The Jews could not have been much worse with no religion at all, than they were under the pressure of their faith in endless torments.

Paul's description of "both Jews and Gentiles," at this period, accords perfectly with the facts adduced, "that they are all under sin; as it is written, There is none righteous, no, not one - there is none that understandeth, there is none that seeketh after God. They are all gone out of the way; they are together become unprofitable; there is none that doeth good, no, not one! Their throat is an open sepulcher; with their tongues they have used deceit; the poison of asps is under their lips; their mouth is full of cursing and bitterness; their feet are swift to shed blood; destruction and misery are in their ways; and the way of peace they have not known; and there is no fear of God before their eyes." Rom. iiI 9-18.

Such is the description of the moral condition of Pagans and Jews, as given by the inspired apostle. How much better were they for having believed in endless punishment? How far were they restrained from sin, or hindered in the indulgence of their evil passions and criminal desires, by the terrors of a future judgment and an endless hell? And yet, in direct contravention of these notorious facts of history, we are told that the doctrine of unending punishment is the only safeguard of society, the great moral force of the world, without which it would speedily fall into irretrievable wreck and ruin! [2]

The truth is, this assumption is entirely barren of facts for its support. There is nothing in history to prove that believers in endless punishment are any better for their faith, or that those denying it are any worse for their want of faith. I do not say, now, that the belief of this doctrine makes people more vicious and wicked, though the last chapter shows that it would not be difficult to demonstrate that this *is* the fact, at least in some respects - but I do say that, so far as history speaks to this point, it gives unmistakable witness that the doctrine of endless torments makes people no more moral, and the absence of it makes them no less moral.

There is a remarkable passage in Wayland's Life of Judson, illustrative of the subject at hand. It relates to the religion and morals of the Burmans, and shows, with singular precision and plainness, the perfect uselessness of the terror system in restraining men from evil, or in promoting their virtue.

Speaking of the Buddhists, he says they believe that mankind pass into other bodies, and the change which then takes place is determined by their conduct in the present life. They may be sent into the bodies of animals, birds, beasts, fish, or insects, from a higher to a lower grade, if wicked, until they reach hell, or to a place of unmixed torment. In cases of atrocious crime, as the murder of a parent, or a priest, they pass through no transmigration, but go directly to hell. "There are four states of misery appropriated to the punishment of atrocious crimes. In the lesser hells are punished those who do not honor their parents, the magistrates, or old age; who take wine and intoxicating drinks; who corrupt wells and destroy highways; who are fraudulent and deceitful, or speak angrily and roughly; who use personal violence, who disregard the words of pious men; who propagate scandal, who injure their fellow-creatures, neglect the sick, or cherish forbidden thoughts. All these will be punished, according to the measure of their sin, with punishments awful beyond conception. For the *least* aberration from rectitude the torment is only less than infinite; and after one sin, the being is forever helplessly under condemnation, unless he can attain to annihilation. It is a pure system of rewards and punishments, without relenting, without pardon, and without hope for the guilty." "Thus," he adds, "this system seems to have exhausted the human faculties in conceiving of terrors which should deter us from sin."

And now what is the result? The Burmans ought to be a very good and holy people, if the doctrine really is as restraining and morally efficacious as is claimed. But what are the facts? Dr. Judson frankly confesses that "this system of religion has no power over the heart, or restraint on the passions;" and Dr. Wayland as frankly owns that it "is found practically to have created no barrier whatever against sin." And the details given by the latter are certainly good proof that these statements are strictly correct and reliable, as the following quotation will satisfactorily show:

"While the law of Gaudama, the Deity, forbids to take the life of any animated being, the Burmans are blood-thirsty, cruel and vindictive, beyond most of the nations of India. Murders are of very common occurrence, and the punishment of death is inflicted with every aggravation of cruelty. While licentiousness is absolutely forbidden, they are said to be universally profligate. While the law denounces covetousness, they are, almost to a man, dishonest, rapacious, prone to robbery, and to robbery ending in blood. The law forbids treachery and deceit on all occasions; and yet, from the highest to the lowest, they are a nation of liars. When detected in the grossest falsehood, they indicate no consciousness of shame, and even pride themselves on successful deceit." [3]

What a complete refutation of the assertion that the fear of hell is an effectual restraint on the wicked passions of men, a moral force essential to the security and well-being of society! Can anything be more conclusive that these facts against this theory? You cannot have a worse hell, nor a worse people, that the Burman. And I do not see how it is possible, in the presence of such unquestionable testimony from history, to persist in the assertion that the belief of endless punishment, or of torments after death, however terrible, is absolutely necessary to the preservation of social order, and as a restraint on the desperate depravity of the human heart.

I turn now to the other side of the subject. It was said that, so far as history goes, those who believed the doctrine of future endless punishment were no better for their faith; and those who rejected it no worse for their want of faith. The first, I think, is proved by unimpeachable testimony. Is it possible to show, in like manner, that those who deny the doctrine are no worse for their want of faith? Let us see what may be done in this regard.

The sect of *Sadducees,* among the Jews, is well known as rejecting the doctrine in review, and even all future existence. Of course, all the frightful descriptions of hell, such as those among the Greeks and Romans and Burmans, went for nothing with them. They had no faith whatever in devils or torments beyond death. All restraints from this source they utterly repudiated, and lived without the slightest reference to any other punishments of sin than such as are administered by the providence of God in this world.

Now, according to the argument of restraint, which affirms that this doctrine is the only safeguard of morals, and that, without it, the vile and dangerous passions of human nature break into a perfect revel of wickedness - if this be true, then we ought to find the Sadducees among the most immoral, corrupt and criminal people of any age or nation. But what is the fact? What is the voice of history? The very reverse of this. And on this point I shall cite the authority of orthodox witnesses, who, however reluctant, are compelled to bear testimony against their own favorite theory.

First, I introduce the statement of Brucker, the distinguished author of the History of Philosophy, which makes the substance of Enfield's work on the same subject.

"It remains," says he, "that we add something concerning the *life* of the Sadducees. It might indeed be conjectured from the character of their doctrine that their life was bad, because they were destitute of those motives by which true morality is enforced. But we must pronounce otherwise concerning their morals, if we adhere to the testimony of the ancients. For Josephus testifies that this class of men was very severe in judging; whence may be inferred their rigor in punishing crimes. This, indeed, is what the nature of their system seems to have required; for, as they did not believe that men were to be deterred from wickedness by the fear of future torments, they were obliged to guard the public morals and observance of the law by rigorous punishments. Josephus himself, though a Pharisee, shows, by a testimony above all exception, that the Sadducees paid a stricter regard to justice than did the Pharisees."

What can be more directly to the point, or more decisive, than this? As respects Josephus, it comes from one of the most distinguished men of the nation, of an opposite sect, an enemy, a Pharisee; and yet the testimony shows the strictness and moral purity of the lives of those men who wholly rejected the popular dogma of future endless punishment!

But let us hear Milman, in his history of the Jews. He says of the Sadducees: "Denying all punishments for crime in a future life, their only way to discourage delinquency was by the immediate terrors of the law; and this they put in force, perhaps with the greater rigor, because their disbelief of future rewards and punishments was represented by their enemies as leading necessarily to the utmost laxity of morals. (The same thing which is affirmed in these days.) This effect it would probably have on many of the weak and licentious; but the doctrine of the Sadducees, which fully recognized the certain punishment of guilt in this world by Divine Providence, is not justly chargeable with these consequences." [4]

Now it is plain enough that these facts and admissions, with regard to the Sadducees, yield the whole question in debate. They are decisive against the asserted necessity and utility of the doctrine in review; decisive in support of the declaration we have so often made, that the opposite faith is not dangerous to the morals of the believer, nor destructive of the good order and well-being of society.

I think the facts adduced establish, beyond refutation, these results:

1st. The belief of future endless torments does not restrain nor prevent men from the indulgence of their criminal passions. Those believing are no better, in character or conduct, *because* they believe it. The hell of the Burmans is as horrible as imagination or invention can make it; and yet they are notoriously corrupt, licentious, bloody-minded - the greatest thieves, liars and cheats in the world.

2d. The disbelief of endless torments does not make man immoral or wicked; as the character of the Sadducees, whom their enemies even acknowledge to be strictly just and moral, abundantly demonstrates.

I can imagine but one reply to this simple statement of facts: It may be said the comparison is not just, since the Burmans, as well as the Greeks and Romans, are heathen, and the Sadducees had the benefit of revelation, and of the divine law of Moses. But this is yielding the point in debate; for the ground taken is, that a religion without the doctrine in question cannot exert a salutary moral influence; that the belief of this is indispensable as a check on the wicked heart. To say, therefore, that other elements of the law, or of revelation, might have made the Sadducees moral and virtuous, is surrendering the argument, and admitting that this doctrine is *not* necessary to virtue.

Still, there is no difficulty in meeting the objection on its own ground. The Greeks, Romans, and Burmans are heathen, but the Pharisees are not. They are believers in divine revelation, having all the benefits of the Law of Moses, living side by side with the Sadducees, subject to the same social influences; the only difference between them being precisely the point in debate - the Pharisees believing the doctrine of future endless punishment, and the Sadducees denying it.

Of course the Pharisees ought to be great saints, without spot or blemish; and the Sadducees ought to be great sinners, vile and wicked to the last degree. But we have already seen that the Sadducees were not great sinners, but honest, just and moral, by confession of their worst enemies. One half the argument, therefore, falls to the ground at the outset. Now for the other half - were the Pharisees great saints? The Savior will answer to this: "Scribes,

Pharisees, hypocrites; robbing the widow and fatherless, neglecting justice, mercy and truth; generation of vipers; whited sepulchers, full of corruption and all manner of uncleanness!" This does not look much like being very saintly. So the second half of the argument fares no better than the first half; and both are perfect failures.

Thus, exactly the reverse of what is claimed for the doctrine proves to be the historical fact: those believing it are great sinners, moral vipers, whited sepulchers; while those disbelieving are - not saints perhaps, but vastly better than the sanctimonious hypocrites, who charged their doctrine with immoral and dangerous tendencies.

One other thing is worthy of note in this connection, and with this I close the argument. In all his rebukes and denunciations of the wickedness of the men of His age and generation, the Savior never includes the Sadducees. It is always, "Scribes, *Pharisees,* hypocrites;" never Scribes, *Sadducees,* hypocrites. This is strong presumptive proof of the unimpeachable morality of the Sadducees, and equally positive proof of the preeminent wickedness of the Pharisees.

We return, therefore, to the conclusion already stated, viz.: The belief of endless punishment does not tighten the bonds of morality, nor lead to a life of virtue; while, on the other hand, the disbelief of it does not loosen the bonds of morality, nor lead to a life of wickedness. [5]

[1] Jewish Wars, Book v., chap. xiii. sect. 6; chap. x. sect. 5.
[2] It is a curious fact that the celebrated work of Bp. Warburton, "The Divine Legation of Moses," has this proposition for its basis: Society cannot exist without a belief in future rewards and punishments; or, in the absence of this, by miraculous support from God. The law of Moses does not contain the doctrine of future rewards and punishments; therefore his legation, or mission, was divine, and the Jewish nation was upheld by the miraculous power of God. This argument he elaborates, with a vast array of learning, and a wonderful display of onesided logic, through three octavo volumes, of more than 1500 closely-printed pages!
[3] Wayland's Life of Judson, vol. I, pp. 144-153.
[4] History of the Jews, vol. ii, pp. 123, 62. Brucker, ii 728, cited in Expositor, iii. 17.
[5] For additional proof see chap. x., sect. vi.

Chapter Nine - The Influence of the Doctrine on the Happiness of Its Believers - Illustrated by Their Confessions

It has seemed to me a fitting conclusion to this work, to show the effect of a belief in endless punishment on the generous mind and really Christian heart, in contrast with the effect of faith in the doctrines of the Gospel, as recorded in the New Testament.

It is impossible that any one, with a human heart in him, can fully believe this doctrine, with all the horrors it involves, with all the accusations it brings against the divine wisdom and goodness, and not feel that it is a terrible weight on his soul, and one from which he would gladly be relieved.

There are many shallow minds, many flippant talkers, who find no difficulty whatever in believing, who are prompt to denounce the slightest doubt on the subject as impiety or infidelity. There are many small ministers, who are ready at a moment's notice to clear up all the difficulties of the moral and scriptural arguments; who are never embarrassed, never troubled at all in regard to the matter.

But I know that the best and strongest among its believers never treat the subject in this way. Those who have looked into it most deeply and patiently, who are distinguished equally for their learning and piety, confess that, seen from any side you will, it is a fearful thing, and leads to anguish of mind, and distress of heart, and to painful questionings which cannot be answered.

The following testimonies are of this class, and they will show, better than any argument, how completely the effects of faith in this dreadful dogma are opposed to the rest, and peace, and joy, promised to the true believer.

SAURIN. This celebrated divine holds the following language: "I sink! I sink under the awful weight of my subject; and I declare, when I see my friends, my relations, the people of my charge, this whole congregation; when I think that I, that you, that we are all threatened with these torments; when I see, in the lukewarmness of my devotions, in the languor of my love, in the levity of my resolutions and designs, the least evidence, though it be presumptive only, of my future misery, yet I find in the thought a mortal poison, which diffuseth itself into every period of my life, rendering society irksome, nourishment insipid, pleasure disgustful, and life itself a cruel bitter. I cease to wonder that the fear of hell hath made some mad, and others melancholy."

Now, can any one suppose for a moment that a doctrine, producing such mental terror and distress as this, can come from Him who said, so kindly and compassionately, "Come unto me, all ye that labor and are heavy laden, and I will give you rest. Take my yoke upon you, and learn of me; for I am meek and lowly in heart; and ye shall find rest unto your souls. For my yoke is easy, and my burden is light"? Matt. xi 29, 30. Besides, He expressly says that He was sent "to preach good tidings, to heal the broken-hearted, to preach deliverance to the captives, and recovering of sight to the blind, and to set at liberty them that are bruised." Luke iv.

PROF. STUART. But to make the contrast still more obvious, I give the following from Rev. Moses Stuart, the late distinguished professor of Andover, equally well known for his critical scholarship and Christian character:

"There are minds of a very serious cast, and prone to reasoning and inquiry, that have in some way come into such a state, that doubt on the subject of endless punishment cannot without the greatest difficulty be removed from them.

"They commence their doubts, it is probable, with some *a priori* reasoning on this subject. 'God is good. His tender mercy is over all the works of his hands. He has no pleasure in the death of the sinner. He has *power* to prevent it. He knew, before he created man and made him a free agent, that he would sin. In certain prospect of his endless misery, therefore, his benevolence would have prevented the bringing of him into existence. No father can bear to see his own children miserable without end, not even when they have been ungrateful and rebellious; and God, our heavenly Father, loves us better than an earthly parent does or can love his children.'

"Besides, our sins are temporary and finite; for they are committed by temporary and finite beings, and in a world filled with enticements both from without and from within. It is perfectly easy for Omnipotence to limit, yea, to prevent, any mischief which sin can do; so that the endless punishment of the wicked is unnecessary, in order to maintain the divine government, and keep it upon a solid basis. Above all, a punishment without end, for the sins of a few days or hours, is a proportion of misery incompatible with justice as well as mercy. And how can this be any longer necessary, when Christ has made atonement for sin, and brought in everlasting redemption from its penalty?

"The social sympathies, too, of some men are often deeply concerned with the formation of their religious opinions. They have lost a near and dear friend and relative by death; one who never made any profession of religion, or gave good reason to suppose that his mind was particularly occupied with it. What will they think of his case? Can they believe that one so dear to them has become eternally wretched - an outcast forever from God? Can they endure the thought that they are never to see or associate with him any more? *Can heaven itself be a place of happiness for them, while they are conscious that a husband or a wife, a son or a daughter, a brother or a sister, is plunged into a lake of fire from which there is no escape?* 'It is impossible,' they aver, 'to overcome such sympathies as these. It would be unnatural and even monstrous to suppress them.' They are, therefore, as they view the case, constrained to doubt whether the miseries of a future world can be endless.

"If there are any whose breasts are strangers to such difficulties as these, they are to be congratulated on having made attainments almost beyond the reach of humanity in the present world; or else to be pitied for ignorance, or the want of a sympathy which seems to be among the first elements of our social nature. With the great mass of thinking Christians, I am sure such thoughts as these must, unhappily for them, be acquaintances too familiar. That they *agitate our breasts as the storms do the mighty deep,* will be testified by every man of a tender heart, and who has a deep concern in the present and future welfare of those whom he loves."

Such a frank and full confession of the difficulties of this question, from such a man, ought to lead all believers to ask, seriously, if it is reasonable to suppose that any doctrine coming from God would lay such a burthen of doubt and suffering on the pious heart and honest mind, or so stand in the way of the perfect trust and love which He requires of us.

And it is of some consequence that those who have lost relatives and friends, giving no evidence of special conversion and regeneration, should consider the question proposed, whether heaven itself can be happiness, if a parent or child, husband or wife, brother or sister, is writhing in a lake of fire from which there is no escape? The believers of this doctrine are very ready to think that those who are dear to them will, somehow, be saved; but, if the doctrine is really true in all its phases, then they who are not truly and actually converted, must inevitably be damned! And if they are not, then the same mercy which saves them may save others, may save all.

BARNES. I add another testimony, which comes from one well known as a man of thought and of sincere piety, ReV Albert Barnes. It is enough to soften a heart of stone into sympathy and pity, to listen to the outburst of anguish with which he acknowledges the crushing effects of this doctrine on mind and heart:

"That the immortal mind should be allowed to jeopard its infinite welfare, and that trifles should be allowed to draw it away from God, and virtue, and heaven. That any should suffer forever, - lingering on in hopeless despair, and rolling amidst infinite torments without the possibility of alleviation, and without end. That since God *can* save men, and *will* save a part, he has not purposed to save *all;* that, on the supposition that the atonement is ample, and that the blood of Christ can cleanse from all and every sin, it is not in fact applied to all. That, in a word, a God who claims to be worthy of the confidence of the universe, and to be a being of infinite benevolence, should make such a world as this, full of sinners and sufferers; and that when an atonement had been made, he did not save *all* the race, and put an end to sin and woe forever:

"These, and kindred difficulties, meet the mind when we think on this great subject; and they meet us when we endeavor to urge our fellow-sinners to be reconciled to God, and to put confidence in him. On this ground they hesitate. These are *real,* not imaginary difficulties. They are probably felt by every mind that ever reflected on the subject; and they are unexplained, unmitigated, unremoved. I confess, for one, that I feel them, and feel them more sensibly and powerfully the more I look at them, and the longer I live. I do not understand these facts; and I make no advances towards understanding them. I do not know that I have a ray of light on this subject, which I had not when the subject first flashed across my soul. I have read, to some extent, what wise and good men have written. I have looked at their theories and explanations. I have endeavored to weigh their arguments, for my whole soul pants for light and relief on these questions. But I get neither; and, in the distress and anguish of my own spirit, I confess that I see no light whatever. I see not one ray to disclose to me the reason why sin came into the world; why the earth is strewed with the dying and the dead, and why man must suffer to all eternity.

"I have never seen a particle of light thrown on these subjects, that has given a moment's ease to my tortured mind; nor have I an explanation to offer, or a thought to suggest, which would be of relief to you. I trust other men - as they profess to do - understand this better than I do, and that they have not the anguish of spirit which I have; but I confess, when I look on a world of sinners and of sufferers; upon death-beds and grave-yards; upon the world of woe, filled with hosts to suffer forever; when I see my friends, my parents, my family, my people, my fellow-citizens; when I look upon a whole race, all involved in this sin and danger, and when I see the great mass of them wholly unconcerned, and when I feel that God only can save them, and yet he does not do it, I am struck dumb. It is all dark, dark, dark to my soul, and I cannot disguise it." [1]

O, can it be that this "tortured mind," this "distress and anguish of spirit," this impenetrable gloom, this wild wail of sorrow, are the natural fruits of faith in God, in Christ, in the Bible? Can it be that a doctrine producing such dreadful effects on the mind and heart of the believer makes a part of the message of the blessed Savior, whose birth was announced by angels as "good tidings of great joy, which shall be unto all people," bringing "peace on earth, and good will toward men"? Luke ii Who can believe this? Who can fail to see the direct opposition in spirit and fact?

HENRY WARD BEECHER. The reader will be interested in the following. It is from one known at home and abroad as one of the most able, eloquent, and wonderful preachers of the present day; and its singular accord with the last, from Barnes, in spirit and in its revelation of anguish and suffering consequent upon belief in this horrible dogma, is worthy of note. It is marvelous that a man of Mr. Beecher's intelligence should allow such passages as that which makes his text to blot out that beautiful and memorable Sermon on the Mount; strange beyond measure that he should suffer such doubtful phraseology to overshadow the Savior's tender invitation to those in sorrow and distress, - "Come unto me all ye that labor and are heavy laden. Take my yoke upon you, and learn of me; for MY *yoke is easy and* MY *burden is light, and ye shall find* REST *unto your souls."* Is it Christ's yoke and Christ's burden that Mr. Beecher is bearing? Has he found the promised rest? Let the following painful confession answer: -

"I have felt every difficulty that any man has ever felt. In my thought I walk around about the terrific fact of the future. I, too, take into account the Fatherhood of God, and I look upon the unpitied nations of the globe, and with inexpressible longing and anguish for which there is no word, I have sought relief. But there is the plain, simple testimony of Jesus Christ. I cannot get around that, nor get over it. There it is. I have nothing to say. I cannot fathom the matter. A child can ask me questions that I cannot answer. I find my soul aching. As it were drops of blood flow for tears. But after all I do believe in the Lord Jesus Christ; and I do not believe he would deceive me nor deceive you. And if you ask me for the reason of the faith that is in me, I simply say this, "Jesus says so:" that is all. And I cannot give up his testimony. I preach the love of God, and I do not know what the scope of that love is; I do not know where it would logically lead. But I am sure that I am right in preaching that all punitive elements are under the control of love. I am perfectly sure that love will bring every thing right in the end. I therefore preach without qualification, and almost without limitation, on that side. But I am not to be understood on that account, as not believing what Christ himself deliberately says in respect to the peril of sin, or in regard to punishment in the life which is to come...

"It goes to my heart to say these things. This is not the side that I seem to myself called to preach. Yet it is there; and, if I am faithful to my whole duty, I must preach it. As a surgeon does things that are most uncongenial to himself, so sometimes I do. And I do this with tears and with sorrow. It makes me sick.

"There is not another teaching of the Bible that comes home to us as does this truth of punishment in the future life. On this subject men cannot keep down the heart while they are coolly weighing the evidence...My brethren, it is one thing to read in the Bible the chapter as I read it in your hearing this morning, and other such passages, and another thing to ponder them in the face of a dead child. It may not be difficult for a theologian to sit in his chair and reason abstractly, rebutting and counter-thrusting in argument; but when he is called to follow his own son, who through a doubtful or an openly-ignominious career has gone out of life, it is not in human nature any longer to reason in the same calm mood. To apply this truth in the intensity of agonized love following its lost companion, like another Orpheus seeking Eurydice, - these are things that bring this question home as almost no other is ever brought home to us.

"If to be born again, if to begin to love, if to hate selfishness, if to begin a separation from our animal nature, are the conditions of joy in the future life, then how few of all the existing people on the globe have met those conditions! And yet I will defy any man to look with a sympathetic heart out upon the masses that are moving more than all the leaves of the forests of the continent, and let the conviction pass his mind as even the shadow of a shade, without being utterly overwhelmed. A man cannot have the susceptibility which is cultivated by the gospel of Christ, and then look boldly in the face the terrific application of this simple truth to the outlaying masses of mankind, and not shiver and tremble with sensibility.

"The *eternity* of punishment, when any thing like a conception of its signification and meaning seizes the mind, seems to paralyze many with grief. The eternity of future punishment is the point where almost all agonizing doubts and struggles of Christian theologians have arisen. And of what are called the *insoluble mysteries of divine government,* it seems to me, that, if the doctrine of the eternity of punishment were removed, nine out of ten would disappear of themselves; for I believe that they result simply from that one term, 'suffering eternity.'"

Such is the confession of this eminent man, and it is equally honorable to his head and his heart. He has the courage to say what, no doubt, thousands of his brethren feel without ever giving it utterance. And Mr. Beecher also has the candor and manliness - speaking of those who have been forced to abandon the awful doctrine as the only way of vindicating the divine character and government, the only way to peace of mind - to bear the following witness: -

"We cannot meet this anguish of men's hearts on cold, exegetical grounds. We may not believe with them; but we cannot denounce them. We may think that they have taken an evasive line of reasoning, or that they have gone off on a fancy, rather than a true line of fact; or we may say that it is contrary to the testimony of Scripture: but when great natures, in the anguish of their souls, and with their sympathies enkindled for their fellow-men, have taken one or the other of these grounds, they are to be respected, and not persecuted...I do not say that they are right or wrong; but this I declare, that, if there is any one point on which we are to be tolerant and charitable and forbearing in our constructions of men's beliefs, it is on this."

DR. PATTON. A single testimony more will close this chapter. "Do you imagine that only Universalists shudder at the idea of eternal ruin of lost souls? All thoughtful men share your dread of the fact, and would gladly reject the doctrine if they honestly could. Nothing prevents me personally from welcoming the doctrine that all will finally be saved, but the want of evidence for it. The Orthodox generally have the same feeling. It pains us to think so many of our fellow-men are living in sin, and dying without hope.

"We have had neighbors, friends, and dear relatives, who have died, giving no evidence of Christian character, but of quite the opposite; and we should be overjoyed, that at last we should all meet above, holy and happy. I frankly acknowledge that it would lift a dark cloud from the world and a heavy load from my heart, could I believe the doctrine.

"The thought is attractive to our reason, that the universe will be in complete harmony with itself; that God will use methods, in the lapse of ages, by which sin and misery shall be terminated, and holiness and happiness characterize all his rational creatures. We can hardly conceive that a good man should be without sympathy with such longings and hopes...Not a few Christians lean decidedly towards this belief. John Frederic Oberlin and John Foster entertained it, after an examination of the subject in the light of reason and the Word of God; while the contrary view is accepted by others only with painful doubt and a sense of conflict."

We commend to Dr. Patton the comforting assurances of the evangelical prophet, which Paul applies directly to the redemption in Christ, in 1 Cor. xv: "And in this mountain (the gospel) shall the Lord make unto all people a feast of fat things;...and he will destroy in this mountain (through the gospel) the covering cast over the face of *all people,* and the veil that is spread over *all nations.* He will swallow up death in victory; and the Lord God will wipe away tears *from off all faces;* and the rebuke of his people shall he take away from off all the earth: for the Lord hath spoken it. And it shall be said in that day, Lo, this is our God; we have waited for him, and he will save us: this is the Lord; we have waited for him, we will be glad, and rejoice in his salvation" (Isa. xxv 6-9).

When this grand prophecy is fulfilled, the "dark cloud" of which Dr. Patton speaks will be "lifted from the world;" and, when he believes this testimony of the Lord, he will throw off the *"heavy load* from his heart," and realize the truth of the Savior's words, *"My* yoke is easy, and *my* burden is *light."*

Let us contrast these records of personal experience with some found in the New Testament, and we shall see the opposition more clearly.

Among the first accounts we have in the book of Acts, it is written, that "all who believed were together, continuing daily with one accord in the temple; and, breaking bread from house to house, did eat their meat with gladness and singleness of heart, praising God, and having favor with all people." Chapter ii

When Philip went down to Samaria, and preached Christ and the Gospel to them, and wrought miracles of mercy in the divine name, "the people with one accord gave heed unto those things which Philip spake, hearing, and seeing the miracles which he did; and there was great joy in that city."

So the Eunuch, whom Philip instructed, when he believed and understood the doctrine, "went on his way rejoicing." Chapter viii.

And so among the heathen; when the Gospel is preached to them, "they are glad, and glorify the word of the Lord;" "the disciples are filled with joy, and with the Holy Ghost," &c. Chapter xiii.

Add to these the often joyous exclamations of the apostles: "We that have believed do enter into rest;" "We have peace with God through our Lord Jesus Christ, and grace wherein we stand, and rejoice in the hope of God's glory;" "Believing, ye rejoice with joy unspeakable and full of glory;" "Rejoice in the Lord alway, and again I say, rejoice;" "O the depth of the riches both of the wisdom and knowledge of God!...For of him, and through him, and to him, are all things: to whom be glory forever!" "And every creature which is in heaven, and on the earth, and under the earth, and such as are in the sea, *and all that are in them,* heard I saying, Blessing, and honor, and glory, and power, be unto Him that sitteth upon the throne, and unto the Lamb forever and ever!" Heb. iv.; Rom. V; 1 Peter I; Rom. xi; Rev. v.

Now, how marked the opposition between these passages, and those from Stuart and Barnes, as regards the effects of faith! Is it possible to believe that the faith is the same in both cases, when the effects are so different? In the one case, we have rest, peace, joy, rejoicing, and religious exultation overflowing the hearts of those who believe; in the other, doubts, anxieties, torture of mind, anguish of heart, and settled religious gloom.

"Doth a fountain send forth at the same place sweet waters and bitter?" We have here, plainly enough, sweet waters and bitter waters, and there must be two fountains. No argument can make this fact more obvious than these manifest contrasts of the effects of faith.

The simple truth is, the doctrine of endless punishment, really believed, understood, and felt in all its horrors, is enough to crush the brain and heart of any man; and we do not wonder that those who allow themselves to think of it, who begin to look into its awful depths, cry out in despair, "It is all dark, *dark,* DARK to my soul, and I cannot disguise it."

Take the single fact, separated from all its concomitants, stripped of all its disguises, and exhibited in its naked and revolting deformity, - the single fact of a human soul made immortal for suffering, kept in being endlessly only that it may be endlessly tormented; compelled to remain in sin, shut out from all possibility of repentance and deliverance, - this is too absolutely horrible for belief, thorough, intelligent belief, without drifting to the very verge of insanity, unless the heart is made of cast-iron.

And, then, when it is remembered that this is under the government of a God who has all resources of wisdom, power, and spiritual influences to prevent it; and who, while permitting and doing this, requires us to adore and love Him with all the heart and soul, it is not possible to keep down a feeling of horror and loathing. It is not possible to love such a God, to worship Him in spirit and in truth, to pray to Him, or praise Him. The whole being revolts at the thought of it. Reason, reverence, affection, all shrink away from Him with undisguised terror and disgust; and, instead of the light and joy of Christian faith, there is nothing for the soul but the darkness of doubt, perpetual unrest, and the agony of despair.

From all this there is but one refuge; and that is, the utter rejection of a doctrine so plainly opposed to the spirit of the Gospel, and to the commandment of faith and love, and the full and hearty reception of the divine truth that God is the Father of all, Christ the Savior of all, and Heaven the final home of all; that all sin and evil shall perish, and good and holiness and happiness be triumphant forever.

> "One adequate support
> For the calamities of mortal life
> Exists, only one, - an assured belief
> That the procession of our fate, however
> Sad or disturbed, is ordered by a Being
> Of infinite benevolence and power,
> Whose everlasting purposes embrace
> All accidents, converting them to good."

[1] Barnes' Practical Sermons, pp. 123-125; Biblical Repository for July, 1840; Saurin's Sermons. See, also, the difficulties and painful struggles created by this doctrine, as they appear in Beecher's Conflict of Ages, and John Foster's celebrated Letter on the subject. *Life and Correspondence,* Letter 226. Beecher's Sermon on Future Punishment, Sunday, Oct. 16, 1870.

Chapter Ten - Additional Testimonies on the Questions Discussed in The Preceding Chapters

Since the publication of the first editions of this work, I have come upon other facts and testimonies illustrating and fortifying the positions taken in the general argument respecting the origin of the doctrine of endless punishment. It has seemed to me that it might add to the value of the book and to the satisfaction of the reader, to gather these up, and present them in an additional chapter of *authorities.*

Still another chapter might be added to the *history* of the doctrine, - a chapter showing the amazing change which has been brought about in all the churches as regards the style and frequency of preaching it. As Henry Ward Beecher justly says, "The educated Christian mind of all lands, for the last hundred years, has been changing; and milder expressions and a very different spirit have prevailed. It is not preached as it used to be, - not as it was in my childhood. It has not been preached as often as, nor with the same fiery and familiar boldness that, it used to be. Multitudes of men who give every evidence of being spiritual, regenerate, and devout, and laborious and self-denying, find themselves straitened in their minds in respect to this question, and are turning anxiously every whither to see whence relief may come to them.' [1] I should be glad to devote a chapter to this interesting, instructive, and prophetic phase of the subject, and emphasize the contrast between the preaching and writing of Calvin, Boston, Edwards, Bellamy, the elder Beecher, Park-street Griffin, and others of the olden times; and Kingsley, Stanley, Brooke, Park-street Murray, and the younger Beechers of to-day. But this must be postponed to another time; my present limits allowing only a place for the chapter of authorities already collected.

Section I. Additions to Chap. II, Sect. II Testimony of Orthodox Critics and Theologians to the Fact That the Doctrine Is Not Taught in the Law of Moses.

LEE, in his "Eschatology," says, "If we refer to the Mosaic institute we shall find that its motives are drawn, not from the future, but from the present world. The rewards of fidelity and the penalties for disobedience were of time and earth...In the Pentateuch we find no motives drawn from the future world. The Old Testament makes no allusion to the *mode of existence* that succeeds the present." Again he says, "It must be remembered that the rewards and punishments of the Mosaic institutes were exclusively temporal.

No allusion is found, in the case of individuals or communities, in which reference is made to the good or evil of a future state as a motive to obedience." [2]

DR. PAYNE SMITH, in his Bampton Lectures, says, "The distinguishing characteristic of prophecy, as it existed in Moses, is that it gives the whole outline of the gospel truth. There is, indeed, one remarkable exception. Moses did not clearly teach the Israelites the doctrine of a future judgment and of an eternal state of rewards and punishments." [3]

REV F.W. FARRAR of Trinity College, Cambridge, Eng., author of the article on "Hell" in Smith's Bible Dictionary, says, "The rewards and punishments of the Mosaic law were temporal; and it was only gradually and slowly that God revealed to his chosen people a knowledge of future rewards and punishments." *Very* slowly, we should think; for the writer himself admits that it was not till after the exile, B.C. 536-445, that the Jews divided *sheol* "into two parts; one the abode of the blessed, and the other of the lost." And even at this he offers not a single scriptural text in proof of the assertion, that at this late date, *a thousand years after the giving of the law,* the Hebrews entertained any such notion of *sheol.* And, even allowing the assertion, it must strike the careful thinker as very strange that God should reveal this doctrine to His chosen people, not directly, but through the Babylonians or Persians, as Mr. Farrar seems to intimate by his allusion to the exile.

DR. STRONG, one of the editors of Harpers' "Cyclopaedia of Biblical and Theological Literature," gives the following testimony: "The Egyptian religion, in its reference to man, was a system of responsibility mainly depending on future rewards and punishment. The law (of Moses), in its reference to man, was a system of responsibility mainly depending on temporal rewards and punishments." [4]

H.W. BEECHER says, "The whole Mosaic economy lies open before us; and there is not one single instance in it where a motive is addressed to a man in consequence of immortality. All the motives are drawn from secular things. Virtue shall bring in this life its reward, and wickedness in this life shall bring its punishment. That is the keynote of that sublime drama of Job."

And he says in another discourse, in substance, that the strangest thing regarding the doctrine of endless punishment is, that, if "we had only the Old Testament, we could not tell if there were any future punishment." [5]

And is it not a strange thing to Mr. Beecher, that God, after four thousand years of silence and concealment, should reveal the horrible thing in that gospel which is declared specially to be "good tidings of great joy unto all people"?

Section II. Additions to Section III of Chap. II Sheol, Or the Old Testament Doctrine of Hell.

DR. FAIRBAIRN, the learned professor of divinity in the College of Glasgow, and whose volumes on "Prophecy" and "Typology" have given him high rank among biblical students and interpreters, says without reserve, "Beyond doubt, *sheol,* like *hades,* was regarded as the abode after death, alike of the good and the bad." Of course, therefore, to translate it by the English word "hell" is to misrepresent the sacred writers, and mislead the common reader.

EDWARD LEIGH, whom Horne, in his "Introduction," says was "one of the most learned men of his time, and his work a valuable help to the understanding of the original languages of the Scriptures," declares unqualifiedly, that "all learned Hebrew scholars know the Hebrews have no proper word for hell, as we take hell."

F.W. FARRAR says that hell is the word generally and unfortunately used by our translators to render the Hebrew *sheol,* - unfortunately, because the English word "hell" is mixed up with numberless associations entirely foreign to the minds of the ancient Hebrews. It would perhaps have been better to retain the Hebrew word *sheol,* or else render it always by "the grave," or "the pit."

Section III. Additions to Chap. IV The Jews Borrowed the Doctrine from The Heathen.

The corruption of the Jewish religion, and the numerous pagan dogmas which had been incorporated into the national creed prior to the time of Christ, are important points in the argument; inasmuch as they show how the way was prepared for the reception of the doctrine of endless punishment into the popular belief. We give place, therefore, to the following additional testimonies under this head.

"Errors of a very pernicious kind," says Dr. Mosheim, "had infested the whole body of the people (Jews). There prevailed among them several absurd and superstitious notions concerning the divine nature, invisible powers, magic, &c., which they had partly brought with them from the Babylonian captivity, and partly derived from the Egyptians, Syrians, and Arabians who lived in their neighborhood." Again he says, "The ancestors of those Jews who lived in the time of our Savior had brought from Chaldaea and the neighboring countries many extravagant and idle fancies which were utterly unknown to the original founders of the nation. The conquest of Asia by Alexander the Great was also an event from which we may date a new accession of errors to the Jewish system, since, in consequence of that revolution, the manners and opinions of the Greeks began to spread among the Jews. Beside this, in their voyages to Egypt and Phoenicia, they brought home, not only the wealth of these corrupt and superstitious nations, but also their pernicious errors and idle fables, which were imperceptibly blended with their own religious doctrines." [6]

"The Hebrews received their doctrine of demons from two sources. At the time of the Babylonish captivity, they derived it from the source of the Chaldaic-Persian magic; and afterward, during the Greek supremacy in Egypt, they were in close intercourse with these foreigners, particularly in Alexandria, and added to the magian notions those borrowed from this Egyptic-Grecian source. And this connection and mixture are seen chiefly in the New Testament. It was impossible to prevent the intermingling of Greek speculations. The voice of the prophets was silent. Study and inquiry had commenced. The popular belief and philosophy separated; and even the philosophers divided themselves into several sects, Sadducees, Pharisees, and Essenes; and Platonic and Pythagorean notions, intermingled with Oriental doctrines, had already unfolded the germ of the Hellenistic and cabalistic philosophy. This was the state of things when Christ appeared." [7]

This witness of the learned and accurate historian is directly to the point, and opens to us the sources of the gross corruption, the false doctrines, and pagan superstitions and fables, which overlaid the simple faith of Moses and the prophets in the days of Christ.

Section IV. Additions to Chap. V, Section IV the Words Eternal, Everlasting, Forever, &c.

The ground taken up to this time, that the Hebrew *olam* and the Greek *aionios* represent a strict eternity, that this is the radical and inherent force of the terms, has been abandoned by Dr. Tayler Lewis, one of the most learned and exact critics of the orthodox school, in a recent dissertation of his in Lange's Commentary. His testimony is as follows: "The preacher, in contending with the Universalist or Restorationist, would commit an error, and, it may be, *suffer a failure in his argument,* should he lay the whole stress of it on the etymological or historical significance of the words *aion, aionios, and attempt to prove, that, of themselves, they necessarily carry the meaning of endless duration."*

Again: he says on the Hebrew word in Eccl. I 3, "This certainly indicates, not an endless eternity in the strictest sense of the word, *but only a future of unlimited length."* On Exod. xxi 16 he says, *"Olam* here would seem to be taken as a hyperbolical term for *indefinite* or unmeasured duration;" and then contrasts it with Deut. xxxii 40, as an example of the immense extremes which the context shows in the use of the word, - *"I live forever,* spoken of God in such a way as to mean nothing less than the absolute or endless eternity. *But it is the subject to which it is applied that forces to this, not any etymological necessity in the word itself."*

This is the very ground we have always taken in regard to this entire class of words, that their meaning depends upon the connection, or the subjects to which they are applied. And Prof. Lewis, after stating that *olam* in Eccl. I 3 (and the same is true of its Greek equivalent *aionios*) "cannot mean forever in the sense of endless duration," very properly adds, that "it may be used for such an idea *when the context clearly demands,* as when it is employed to denote the continuance of the divine existence, or of the divine kingdom." Again: he says on chap. xii 5, where the Hebrew of "long home" is *beth olam,* "it certainly does not denote an absolute endless eternity."

The proper meaning of the words, according to the professor, is *world-time;* "First, as expressive of some great period, cycle, or age, not having its measurement from without, but which goes beyond any known historical or astronomical measurement;" second, "in a lower or more limited sense, - an olam, eon, age, world, or world-time, - which may be historical; indefinite periods coming one after another during the continuance of the same earth or *kosmos.* Thus we say the *ancient world,* the *modern world,* the *Greek world,* the *Roman world,* &c. This would correspond to our use of the word 'ages,' and that would make a good sense, Eccl. I 10, 'the worlds or ages that have been before.'"

On Matt. xxv 46 he says, *"Aionios* may perhaps mean an existence, a duration, measured by eons or worlds (taken as the measuring unit), just as our present world, or eon, is measured by years or centuries. But it would be more in accordance with the plainest etymological usage to give it simply the sense of *olamic* or *eonic,* or to regard it as denoting, like the Jewish *olam habba,* the *world to come.* These shall go away into the punishment (the restraint or imprisonment) of the world to come; and these, into the life of the world to come. That is all we can etymologically or exegetically make of the word in this passage."

Section V. Additions to Chap. VI The Introduction of the Doctrine into the Christian Church

The importance of the subject presented in this chapter will justify the additional proofs which follow. No one familiar with the internal history of the Church in the centuries immediately following the apostolic age will require any farther proof than this knowledge will afford him, that it was scarcely possible that the dogma of endless punishment should not find its way into such a mass of superstition and wickedness, such a sink of theological and moral corruption. The following is from an article in the Contemporary Review on "The Corruption of Christianity by Paganism:" -

"That a vast revolution actually took place in very many of the doctrines, and in all the external usages, of the Church, between the age of Constantine and that of Justinian, is simply a matter of history. The truth is too patent to be denied, account for it how we will. The explanation which seems most probable is that which ascribes the change in Christianity to its gradual fusion with the Paganism of the empire.

"The revolution had, like most others, various predisposing causes, which long wrought in silence before their effect became visible. Three are enough to mention: The irresistible tendency of the age towards superstition; the familiar intercourse between the heathen populace and the lower order of Christians; and, lastly, the credulity and false philosophy of most of the learned Christian divines, and their well-meant but mistaken policy in dealing with corruptions introduced by the ignorant. The condition of the Roman world from the very beginning of Christianity was extremely unpropitious to the preservation of its purity; and, as the ancient civilization declined through misgovernment and social disorganization, it became increasingly difficult for the Church to struggle against the mischievous influences that beset her on every side.

"No doubt many Pagan customs were adopted without any bad intention, or, as in the recommendation of Gregory the Great to Augustine of Canterbury, with the good object of winning the heathen to the gospel. The ceremonial and legendary system of Paganism had many romantic charms which are still retained by them under their Christian dress. But, though some admixture of Pagan ideas and practices might be innocently tolerated, it is quite another matter when we see a vast structure of errors, such as apostles and martyrs died to withstand, superadded to the faith once delivered to the saints." [8]

The facts which are gathered into the note below are painful enough; but it is necessary to give place to them in order that the inquirer may fully understand how so abominable a doctrine as that of endless punishment, and so hostile to the spirit of the gospel, should have found its way into the creed of the Christian Church. [9]

Section VI. Additions to Chap. VIII The Comparative Moral Influence of Belief and Disbelief in Endless Punishment. Historical Contrast.

A great many assertions have been made regarding the necessity of a belief in future endless punishment as the safeguard of society, and the only sure foundation of public and private morality. The facts set forth in the chapter to which this section is an appendix show how little ground there is for such assertions; and the history of Pagan nations and tribes everywhere, and in all ages, furnishes the same evidence on this point. No greater wickedness, no more thorough corruption of morals and manners, no more loathsome customs and practices, exist on the earth, than among those very heathen who believe in hells and torments as horrible as language can describe.

But the Christian Church itself also bears witness to the same truth. So long as it was faithful to the doctrines of Christ and to the divine spirit of His gospel, the believers lived according to the law of love and holiness, and honored their profession by the purity of their conversation and conduct. And, as Luke says, "They did eat their meat with gladness and singleness of heart, praising God, and having favor with all the people" (Acts ii). But no sooner do we find a departure from the great truths of Christianity, - the fatherhood of God, the brotherhood of man, the final redemption of all, - than we find a corresponding laxity of morals and looseness of manners; and this increasing with every new remove from the purity of the gospel. The historians of the Church testify with one voice to this corruption and depravity.

"After our affairs degenerated from the rules of piety, one pursued another with open contumely and hatred; and we fought each other with armor of spite, with sharp spears of opprobrious words: so that bishops against bishops, and people against people, raised sedition. Last of all, when that cursed hypocrisy and dissimulation had swum to the brim of malice, the heavy hand of God's judgment came upon us, at first little by little. But when we were not moved by sense or feeling thereof, nor sought to pacify God, but heaped sin upon sin, thinking God would not care or visit us for our sins; and when our shepherds, laying aside the rules of piety, contended and strove violently among themselves, and added strife to strife, and threatenings, mutual hatred and enmity, and tyrannical ambition, - then Jehovah poured his wrath upon us, and remembered us not." [10]

"Although examples of primitive piety and virtue were not wanting, yet many were addicted to dissipation, arrogance, voluptuousness, contention, and other vices. This appears distinctly from the frequent lamentations of the most credible persons of those times." "The presbyters imitated the example of their superiors, and, neglecting the duties of their office, lived in indolence and pleasure." Again: "The vices and faults of the clergy, especially those who officiated in large and opulent cities, were augmented according to their wealth, honors, and advantages. The bishops trampled on the rights of the people and inferior clergy, and vied with the civil governors of provinces in luxury, arrogance and voluptuousness." [11]

Such the moral results following the growth in the Church of the dogma of endless punishment, or the attempt to drive men, through fear of hell, into a life of purity and goodness. And this state of things grew worse and worse, if possible, through that long dismal period so justly described as the "dark ages."

And now let us take another standpoint, and see what presents itself on the other side. Within the last half-century, there has been a great change in the theology of the Church, a wonderful softening-down of the harsh features of all creeds, and a steady approach once more to the simple and sublime doctrines of the gospel. The great truths of Universalism - the parental character and love of God, the brotherhood of man, and the final restoration of all to holiness and blessedness - have, in the last fifty years, made unparalleled progress in America and Europe; and hundreds of thousands rejoice in the knowledge and faith of them; while hundreds of thousands more in churches of every name have already wholly or mostly abandoned the revolting dogma of endless woe.

And now what is the moral condition of society at the present time in America and Europe, compared with that of the period already alluded to, when the principle of brute force and terror prevailed in religion and governments, and the doctrine of interminable torment ruled the Church and the people? Have the people grown worse, or better? Have the moral and human aspects of society brightened, or darkened, under the influence? Let the history of the present answer.

Look abroad upon the noble philanthropic enterprises which are rousing the nations to a new and higher life. Behold the asylums for the insane, the blind, the deaf and dumb; hospitals for the sick and maimed; temperance societies; associations for the employment and relief of the poor; asylums for aged men and women; Odd Fellowship, and kindred associations recognizing and reducing to practice the great principles of human brotherhood, and the duties of mutual love and aid; associations for Christianizing our laws; peace societies; prison-discipline societies; the extension of education; the increase of Christian liberality and toleration, &c.

Do these things indicate a forward, or a retrograde movement? Do these noble reforms, these Christian enterprises of benevolence and humanity, look as if the morals of society were on the decline? Do they show that the wide diffusion of the doctrines of Universalism has had a dangerous influence on public morals? Or, in other words, do these things show that the growing doubts and disbelief of endless punishment, and all its kindred errors, have taken away any salutary restraint, or opened the way to a general violation of Christian and social laws? Are the people of America or Europe worse now than in the dark ages? less enlightened, less virtuous, less Christian, less charitable and loving toward their fellows, less earnest in their efforts to elevate the moral and social condition of the poor and ignorant and degraded, and to set the oppressed and captive free?

To all these questions the uniform and emphatic answer is *No!* So far from society growing worse under these influences, it is hourly growing better. Its moral life is more and more developed; and there has never been a period in the political, social, and religious history of the world, when there were signs of greater promise than now; never a time when there were at work more elements of improvement and progress, or when the present and the future looked more hopeful of good than at this hour. [12]

[1] Sermon on Future Punishment, preached Oct. 16, 1870.
[2] Eschatology; or, the Scriptural Doctrine of the Coming of the Lord, the Judgment, and the Resurrection. By Samuel Lee, Boston, 1859, pp. 6, 144-150.
[3] Prophecy a Preparation for Christ. By R. Payne Smith, D.D., Professor of Divinity, Oxford. Boston, 1870, p. 217.
[4] Cyclopaedia, Art. "Egypt." Dr. Strong says, that not only Moses, but "every Israelite who came out of Egypt, must have been fully acquainted with the universally-recognized doctrine of future rewards and punishments." And yet Moses and Aaron, priest and Levite, are all as silent as *sheol* on the subject.
[5] Sermon on Heaven, Sunday, Oct. 11, 1870. - *Tribune and World Reports.*

[6] Mosheim's Church History, century I pt. I chap. ii See also Guizot's note in Milman's Gibbon, chap. xxi Neander's History, I pp. 49-62.

[7] Encyclopedia Americana, art. "Demon."

[8] Reprinted in Littell's Living Age for April 23, 1870. Other testimonies may be seen in Mosheim, I 115, 125, &c.; Enfield's Hist. Phil. ii 271, 281, &c., and in Church historians generally.

[9] The great ecclesiastical historian, Eusebius, heads chap. xxxi of Book 12 of his Evangelical Preparation thus: "HOW FAR IT MAY BE PROPER TO USE FALSEHOOD AS A MEDICINE, AND FOR THE BENEFIT OF THOSE WHO REQUIRE TO BE DECEIVED." And he undertakes to defend the propriety of using falsehood by appealing to pretended examples in the Old Testament. Origen avowed the same principle (*Mosheim's Dissertations,* p. 203). Bishop Horsley, in his controversy with Dr. Priestley, states the same fact. At page 160, he says, "Time was, when the practice of using unjustifiable means to serve a good cause was openly avowed; and Origen himself was among its defenders." Chrysostom, Bishop of Constantinople, defended the same doctrine (*Mosh. Diss.,* p. 205). Gregory of Nazianzen (A.D. 360-390), surnamed "the Divine," says, "A little jargon is all that is necessary to impose on the people. The less they comprehend, the more they admire. Our forefathers and doctors of the Church have often said, *not what they thought, but what circumstances and necessity dictated to them." Synesius* (A.D. 400-420), Bishop of Ptolemais, says, *"The people are desirous of being deceived. We cannot act otherwise respecting them."* And a little further on he says, "For my own part, to myself I shall always be a philosopher; but in dealing with the mass of mankind I shall be a priest" (*Cave's Eccl.* p. 115). *St. Jerome* (A.D. 380) says, "I do not find fault with an error which proceeds from hatred towards the Jews, and pious zeal for the Christian faith" (*Opera,* iV p. 113). Mosheim "especially includes in the same charge" *Ambrose* (A.D. 270), Bishop of Milan, *Hilary,* Bishop of Poitiers, and *Augustine* (A.D. 400), Bishop of Hippo, "whose fame," says Mosheim, "filled, not without reason, the whole Christian world. We would willingly," he adds, "except them from this charge; but truth, which is more respectable than these venerable fathers, obliges us to involve them in the general accusation." Dr. *Chapman,* in his Miscellaneous Tracts, p. 191, says, "The learned Mosheim, a foreign divine, and zealous advocate for Christianity, who by his writings has deserved the esteem of all good and learned men, intimates his fears, that those who search with any degree of attention into the writings of the fathers and most holy doctors of the fourth century *will find them all, without exception, disposed to lie and deceive whenever the interests of religion require it."* The learned *Dodwell,* in a work published by him, "abstains from producing more proofs of ancient Christian forgeries," "through his great veneration for the goodness and piety of the fathers." What a strange and inconsistent reason was this! - *Universalist Book of Reference,* p. 359.

[10] Eusebius (died A.D. 340), Eccl. Hist. lib. viii. chap. 1.

[11] Mosheim's Eccl. Hist. centuries iii., iv. Murdock's Translation.

[12] For further evidence that the doctrine of endless punishment does not improve the morals of its believers, or restrain the appetites and passions, we refer to a little volume, entitled "Orthodoxy as It Is," chap. iv., containing a record which we are reluctant to transfer to these pages.

CPSIA information can be obtained
at www.ICGtesting.com
Printed in the USA
BVHW081925060723
666786BV00006B/211

9 781789 872293